School art: what's in it?

Exploring visual arts in secondary schools

Dick Downing
Ruth Watson

Published in November 2004 by the National Foundation for Educational Research, The Mere, Upton Park, Slough, Berkshire SL1 2DQ.

© NFER 2004
Registered Charity No. 313392
ISBN 1 903880 87 4

Designed by Stuart Gordon at NFER.
Picture research by Gillian Wilson at Tate.

Cover photograph: David Bebber, 25 October 2003.

Image 1. Andrew Thomson. Digital pupil art

Image 2. David Shrigley Terrible News – no more treats! From 'Blank Page and Other Pages', 1998 © the artist

Image 3. Richard Billingham Untitled, 1995 © the artist

Image 4. Vincent Van Gogh Van Gogh's Bedroom at Arles, 1889 Art Institute of Chicago

Image 5. Damien Hirst The Physical Impossibility of Death in the Mind of Someone Living, 1991 © the artist. Courtesy Jay Jopling/White Cube (London). Photo: Anthony Oliver

Image 6. Andy Warhol Marilyn x 100, 1962 The Cleveland Museum of Art © The Andy Warhol Foundation for the Visual Arts, Inc./ARS, NY and DACS, London 2004-10-29. TM 2004 Marilyn Monroe, LLC by CMG Worldwide, Inc./www.MarilynMonroe.com

Contents

Foreword	v
Acknowledgements	vi
Executive summary	vii
1 Introduction	**1**
1.1 Background to the research	1
1.2 Methodology	2
1.3 The structure of the report	8
2 The content of the art curriculum in secondary schools	**10**
2.1 Introduction	10
2.2 The structure of the school art curriculum at key stage 3 and 4	10
2.3 The content of art modules and schemes of work, as delivered by secondary school art teachers	17
2.4 Other curriculum features	33
2.5 The nature and status of contemporary art practice within school art	39
2.6 Summary and conclusions	49
3 Factors influencing the choice of art curriculum content	**53**
3.1 Introduction	53
3.2 Perceptions of the enabling or inhibiting effects of the nationally prescribed art curriculum	54
3.3 The school context	56
3.4 The art department context	57
3.5 Resource influences	62
3.6 Factors associated with individual teachers	64
3.7 Teacher responses to a selection of art images	70
3.8 Summary and conclusions	80

4	**The perceived impact of contemporary art practice in the secondary school art curriculum**	**84**
4.1	Introduction	84
4.2	The perceived outcomes of the art curriculum	84
4.3	The outcomes of art programmes that include contemporary art practice	92
4.4	Summary and conclusions	100
5	**Implication for policy and practice in visual art teaching**	**103**
5.1	Introduction	103
5.2	The context within which art curriculum choices are made	103
5.3	Questions raised from the research process	106
5.4	Contribution to the body of research into visual art learning in schools	113
5.5	Possible future strategies to address issues concerning art curriculum content	114
	Appendix 1 Research into visual arts learning: a literature review	**117**
	Appendix 2 Images used during research	**144**
	References	**146**
	Further reading	**149**

Foreword

Over the last 20 years the visual arts department has supported projects that promote learning about and through contemporary art: artist in schools initiatives, teacher development programmes, touring exhibitions and curriculum resources. The Arts Council, in association with Tate, commissioned this research to look at what is currently happening in the school art curriculum, and to explore the potential of contemporary arts practice to make a distinctive contribution to the curriculum. For teachers and young people to engage with the expanded field of contemporary art alongside more traditional fine art, is to harness the power of visual culture. This research raises fundamental questions on the meaning, value and purpose of art and opens opportunities to drive the curriculum forward.

Marjorie Allthorpe-Guyton, Director Visual Arts, Arts Council England

Tate's mission is to increase public knowledge, understanding and appreciation of art through an innovative and authoritative range of changing displays, exhibitions, education programmes, publications and events. A key element of Tate's role in showing the work of international contemporary artists is to support young people in engaging with visual culture. As such it is important that pupils' experience of the art curriculum in schools includes contemporary art practice. Our interest in jointly commissioning this research with the Arts Council England is to support teachers and the education sector in the development of the curriculum. It is important that the schools sector and Tate work together to bring an understanding of contemporary visual art to young people. This research will provide vital evidence to shape our enterprise.

Nicholas Serota, Director, Tate

Acknowledgements

The authors would like to thank all the art teachers, heads of departments and pupils who gave us their valuable time throughout the fieldwork phase of the research. The study would not have been possible without them.

We would also like to acknowledge the vital contribution of the Arts Council England (ACE), Tate and the National Foundation for Educational Research (NFER), who not only funded the study but also lent experience, knowledge and insight to it. We would particularly like to thank the steering group members, Toby Jackson, Helen Charman and Tina Melbourne of Tate and Vivienne Reiss of ACE, for their support throughout the research process. We are additionally grateful to members of the steering group for their help in identifying, for inclusion in our study, schools that incorporate contemporary art practice in their curriculum.

We would like to acknowledge the valuable contributions made by Nicola Bedford in conducting some of the fieldwork and assisting with the data processing.

We would also like to thank John Harland, Head of NFER Northern Office, who contributed to the design of the research and gave invaluable advice throughout the process.

Finally we would like to thank Hilary McElderry, Ann Black and Julie Thompson for their secretarial support throughout the project.

Executive summary

Background

This report presents the findings from a year long study designed to ascertain the content of the art curriculum at key stage 3 and 4, with particular reference to the inclusion of contemporary art practice. It was sponsored by the NFER and ACE in association with Tate. Both ACE and Tate have an interest in promoting the role of contemporary art in education.

The research sought to address three main objectives:

- to portray the salient contents and foci of 'school art' at key stage 3 and 4, including a depiction of any programmes involving contemporary art practice
- to identify factors and strategies that inhibit and facilitate the inclusion of contemporary art practice in the school curriculum
- to explore the potential of contemporary art practice to make a distinctive contribution to the art curriculum and pupils' learning.

Methodology

A review of research that addressed the content of the school art curriculum was conducted by NFER librarians, and revealed more literature concerning the aims and effects of art teaching than about the content of the curriculum.

The main body of the research was based entirely on qualitative methods. The sample comprised art departments in ten randomly selected schools and in eight other schools, identified by the sponsors and their nominees, as known to incorporate contemporary art practice in their curriculum (referred to throughout as the CAP identified schools). The research proceeded with no pre-agreed definition of what constitutes contemporary art practice, since there was an intention to leave the term open to interpretation by interviewees.

In each of the sample schools, interviews were carried out with the head of the art department and with a number of their colleagues, depending on the size of the department. In total, 54 art teaching staff were interviewed. They were questioned about curriculum design and content, and their perceptions of the factors affecting curriculum choice. Their perceptions of the outcomes of the art curriculum in their schools were also elicited. Part of each interview involved a detailed description of one specific art module for one year group. On average, each year group was covered in 12 interviews through this method, with an average of three year groups covered in each department. Sixty-two modules were described. Most of the art teachers were also asked to respond to a sample of six images, depicting artworks from a range of artists, as a way of further understanding their thought processes in selecting curriculum content. Teachers in the CAP identified schools were questioned further concerning the inclusion of contemporary art practice in their curricula.

All interviews were recorded and extensively summarised. Data reporting includes rudimentary response frequencies combined with descriptive and perceptual data from interviews, using quotes where appropriate. It is readily acknowledged that the sample size for this research was not large. However, the data is rich and in many respects detailed, and while not presuming to be representative, it is presented in a way that is intended to be both indicative and illustrative.

The content of the curriculum

Descriptions of modules in the randomly identified schools indicate certain prevalent characteristics including:

- the use of painting and drawing as the medium in which pupils work
- the use of artistic references from the early 20th century
- limited use of artistic references from pre-1800 and from the latter 20th and early 21st century
- the prevalent use of male, European artists, predominantly painters
- the importance placed on development of art form skills, including the use of art materials, the development of specific techniques and observational drawing skills.

The following characteristics were more likely to be reported in the CAP identified cohort of schools:

- pupils produced work using information and communications technology (ICT) and other, less traditional media

- teachers used artistic reference from the latter 20th and early 21st century to support the curriculum
- international art/culture and the work of women artists were included in the artistic references used to support the curriculum
- teachers included a wide range of art forms (not only contemporary) in the references used to support the curriculum
- pupils were encouraged to make art to explore issues or express meaning
- teachers encouraged pupils to use and develop creative thinking processes
- the curriculum included visits to galleries and museums and included the use of external artists.

Such characteristics may be more indicative of schools with a broad and eclectic approach to cultural references and the purposes for teaching art, than of schools that include contemporary art practice. Contemporary art practices did not displace more typical approaches to art teaching, but rather complemented them.

Factors influencing the choice of curriculum content

It might be argued that, given the massive potential range of artists and art images available for inclusion in the curriculum for school art, the actual choices made are somewhat limited. This research indicated evidence of a number of factors that influence the choices made.

- Most art teachers did not see guidelines and requirements at national and school level as restrictive, but rather that they supported teachers in choosing curriculum content to suit their own skills and interests.
- However, both department documentation and interviewee discourse revealed a very prevalent orthodoxy that the teaching of art form skills at key stage 3 precedes a move towards more exploratory and independent learning at key stage 4.
- Specific resource factors were perceived to inhibit curriculum content choices, namely space, the availability of materials, art images or computers, access to galleries and/or artist studios and time. Of these, space was the most widely cited inhibitor, affecting teachers in CAP and randomly identified schools equally.

- However, teachers in randomly identified schools were more than twice as likely to cite shortages of time and resources as inhibitors.
- Personal preference was easily the most frequently cited factor affecting teachers' choice of art images for inclusion in the curriculum.
- The capacity of an image to support the learning of art form skills appeared to take precedence over their value in terms of content and meaning.
- There appeared to be evidence of a slow-changing orthodoxy in the choice of curriculum content, with some teachers continuing to include certain images even though they saw them as boring or over-exposed.
- Staff in CAP identified schools were more likely to have worked as professional artists before entering teaching, and thus may be able to share a more thorough understanding of the art production process with their pupils.
- There appeared to be a scarcity of courses in art or art teaching for practising teachers. Courses related to GCSE examinations, especially concerning assessment, comprised the majority of Continuing Professional Development (CPD) opportunities for both teachers and heads of departments.
- In describing their curriculum approach, heads of department in CAP identified schools were more likely to focus on pupil experience, the importance of ideas, current events and external stimuli (such as gallery exhibitions).

The perceived value of the art curriculum and the particular contribution that contemporary art practice might make to it

Teachers in both cohorts of schools were most likely to cite the acquisition of art form skills and knowledge, increased knowledge in the social and cultural domains and personal and social development as the main outcomes of art education in their schools.

Teachers in the CAP identified schools gave the following reasons for choosing to incorporate contemporary art practice in their curriculum:

- to provide a curriculum that is more interesting, relevant and accessible to the pupils.
- to increase pupils' understanding of the wider art world and challenge the notion, 'what is art?'.
- to allow individual teacher preference for contemporary genres to be reflected in the curriculum they taught.

Those teachers suggested that the inclusion of contemporary art practice enhanced the more general effects of art education in the following ways:

- broadening an understanding of what constitutes art form knowledge and skills, and the definition of art itself
- heightening awareness of the relevance of art to pupils' own lives and the subsequent effect this has on their motivation and enthusiasm for studying and creating artwork
- encouraging creativity and thinking skills, particularly the development of pupils' lateral thinking skills
- widening knowledge in the social and cultural domain, primarily the increased understanding of social, environmental and citizenship issues through the study of issue-based art images
- supporting communication and expressive skills, primarily increased visual communication skills through the study of art for meaning.

Implications for policy and practice in visual art teaching

The findings indicate variations in approach between teachers. The following questions are for further consideration.

- Is a wider range of artistic genres or cultural references necessary for a more effective art education?
- Does the apparent concentration on painting and drawing exclude other media such as sculpture, design and photography, and what are the educational repercussions of this?
- Are critical analysis, issue-based learning and the communication of meaning in and through art sufficiently integrated and balanced with the acquisition of the skills of art making?
- Is the limited creative use of ICT in art, as opposed to its use for art research, a shortcoming, given the emphasis placed on the use of ICT within the curriculum as a whole?
- Is sufficient attention being paid in art to the teaching of research skills, and in particular the critical use of the internet?
- Is contemporary art practice an appropriate component of the school art curriculum and can it be accessed effectively for inclusion in the school art curriculum?

- Would the inclusion of contemporary art practice help to address the wider aims of the national curriculum for art (as defined in QCA documents)?
- Is contemporary art practice intellectually, emotionally and socially accessible to students in school?
- Are teachers equipped with the knowledge and understanding to incorporate contemporary art practice in their teaching?
- Is the freedom of choice of teachers to define art curriculum content an appropriate method of selecting the cultural and artistic references to be included?

1 Introduction

1.1 Background to the research

Teaching and learning in the visual arts take place in two distinct contexts: the context of the education system, and the context of a wider world of art production, exhibition and consumption. Within education, the context is defined by timetables, resources, space and expertise. The wider art context is defined by, amongst other things, market forces, societal changes, media coverage and the artists need to explore and expand boundaries. This has resulted in sometimes rapid and sometimes gradual changes in the body of art being produced. The centuries have therefore generated almost limitless possibilities for what could be studied as art in schools. The choice of what should be studied and how it should be studied have generated warm debate for many years. Learning the craft of making art, learning about art and learning through art have all co-existed for some time, although sometimes uncomfortably. It is perhaps surprising then that little research has taken place concerning the actual content of the art curriculum as it is taught in schools.

This report presents the findings of a year long study designed to ascertain the content of the art curriculum at key stage 3 and 4, with a particular reference to the inclusion of contemporary art practice.

While the National Curriculum documentation from the Qualification and Curriculum Authority (QCA) concerning art education, and the syllabuses provided by the various examination boards specify learning areas and objectives, school art departments and individual art teachers have considerable freedom in determining the details of what their pupils will study and experience in their art lessons. They decide what media their pupils will explore and which artists, art forms and cultural references are studied or used as examples in art lessons.

There has been little research to ascertain how school art departments and individual teachers set about making these decisions, or what conclusions they reach. ACE and Tate became aware that efforts to promote the inclusion of contemporary art practice needed to be better informed by an understanding of the context of what is currently happening in the school art curriculum. But the actual content of art lessons has not been the subject of systematic research.

A second impetus for the study came out of an assertion that 'those at the cutting edge of art education perceive that there is a pervading orthodoxy in art and design education resulting in school art which makes little reference to contemporary art in the 21st century' (research background paper, ACE, 2003, unpublished).

Both ACE and the four centres of Tate, had previously identified the need to promote the value of learning in, through, and about the contemporary visual arts and had recognised the need for increased promotion of contemporary art practice in education.

To this end ACE, along with Tate and the NFER, commissioned this research, which sought to address three main objectives.

- Portray the salient contents and foci of school art at key stage 3 and 4, including a depiction of any programmes involving contemporary art practice.
- Identify factors and strategies that inhibit and facilitate the inclusion of contemporary art practice in the school curriculum.
- Explore the potential of contemporary art practice to make a distinctive contribution to the art curriculum and pupils' learning.

1.2 Methodology

1.2.1 The literature review

The project started with a review of the relevant existing literature on research carried out in England since the introduction of the National Curriculum in 1989. The review focused on studies of the content of the school art curriculum as implemented, especially that provided at key stage 3 and 4. The review was based on sources identified by a systematic search of databases of research literature in education and the social sciences by the NFER library in Slough.

1.2.2 Summary of literature review

The literature searches conducted found only a limited selection of research concerned specifically with the curriculum content of secondary school art. A substantial amount of research considers the place of the arts as a whole within the school curriculum but there is little evidence of the form this teaching takes or the content of the curriculum delivered. However, the documents reviewed did reveal relevant issues about the teaching of art, which may have implications for the art curriculum as a whole and the inclusion of contemporary practices.

Three key questions were posed for the literature review.

- What is school art at key stage 3 and 4?
- What are its main foci and contents?
- In what ways are pupils encouraged to broaden their approaches to the process of engaging with art forms and genres?

The findings within the literature relating to a definition of school art are limited. The National Curriculum requirements and associated guidelines, including QCA documentation, can be seen, to an extent, as the defining documentation on what school art is. Key stage 4 art and design curricula are defined by the schools' chosen examining boards' programmes of study. Both GCSE and QCA documentation tend to be objective-based rather than content and foci specific. There was a general consensus that, within the literature, time limitations were causing the arts to be taught through knowledge and skills-based approaches, with the distinct possibility that more conceptual approaches and notions of creativity were being neglected (Ross and Kamba, 1997; Hargreaves and Lamont, 2002).

Very little empirical evidence has been gathered to ascertain the main foci and content of school art beyond the QCA guidelines and suggested schemes of work. These are limited in their specific inclusion of contemporary mediums such as ICT and digital photography, as well as the exploration of contemporary art works. However, these are only guidelines, and the selection of curriculum content to meet the National Curriculum objectives is open to teachers' individual discretion. Literature focusing on the inclusion of contemporary art practice primarily addressed stand-alone projects and did not include researched strategies for the long-term inclusion of contemporary art. From these studies it would seem that the inclusion of ICT as a medium in which pupils' work was the main way in which teachers incorporate contemporary art practice within the key stage 3 and 4 art curriculum.

In answer to the third question, the research reviewed focused more on the types of media in which pupils work, rather than on the processes involved in engaging with them.

In addition to these three key questions the literature review sought to ascertain perspectives on the inclusion of contemporary art, including barriers to its inclusion and perceptions of the learning effects and outcomes of programmes involving contemporary art practice.

Censorship, the sensitivity of issues in contemporary art and the culture of individual schools, were all cited as potential barriers to the inclusion of contemporary art (Emery, 2002; Burgess, 2003; Hutchinson, 1998). In addition, lack of space, resources and time were cited as preventing teachers from researching or accessing training in the use of those resources that were available (Callow, 2001; Sinker, 2001; Loveless, 2003; Rogers and Bacon, 2002). Opposing views on the restrictive nature of the National Curriculum and associated guidelines were revealed. Binch (1994), Pringle (2002), Long (2001) and Hughes (1998) all cite rigid curriculum structures, prioritisation of the core subjects and general constraints on time for art teaching, as key factors that may be limiting the freedom for innovative and contemporary work. However, Hulks (2003) and Burgess (2003) both highlight the flexibility within the National Curriculum, in particular, the way in which it was designed to be a flexible framework in which teachers could develop their own ideas. They suggest that any restrictions on the art studied and the pedagogies employed at secondary level are not as a result of the curriculum itself but of the way in which it has been interpreted.

Whilst the benefits of its inclusion are recognised, the studies are consistent in their opinion that contemporary art, in the present educational system, is not as easily accessible or adaptable for classroom practice as more traditional genres.

Harland *et al.* (2000) proposed a typology of pupil effects derived from the study of the arts (including visual arts) in secondary schools as a whole, as a result of an indepth study into the effects and effectiveness of secondary school arts teaching. No such empirical research was identified concerning the pupil effects of programmes involving contemporary art practice. The perceived learning outcomes of studying contemporary art emerged from evaluations of action research and through discussion papers. These perceptions centred on the potential that contemporary art afforded conceptions of what art is for developing students. The benefits are also perceived in terms of how contemporary practice can improve students' critical awareness and conceptual thinking, as opposed to their art skills or their ability to produce 'good' art. In addition, positive effects of programmes involving contemporary art practice also focused on the opportunities provided in contemporary pieces for the exploration of social, moral and political issues and recognition of art as a visual communication tool (Sinker, 2001; Emery, 2002b; Burgess, 2003).

The full version of the literature review and details of the search strategy employed can be found in Appendix 1, which reports the findings of the review.

1.2.3 Interviews with art teachers and heads of departments

The second phase of the research was based entirely on qualitative methods. Since the intention was to explore the content of the curriculum in considerable detail, it was felt that a survey approach involving questionnaires would be inappropriate. Researcher visits to the art departments in a sample of 18 schools would permit the kind of detailed and considered responses of teachers that form-filling would be unlikely to elicit.

The sample comprised of art departments in ten randomly selected schools and art departments in eight schools identified as incorporating contemporary art practice in their curriculum. Of these, three were selected to visit for an extended period in order to undertake additional interviews and observation. For the most part, these three schools will be included for analysis purposes in the cohort henceforth referred to as the CAP identified schools.

The sample of ten schools were randomly selected from across England and consisted of four in the south (including one in London), five in the north and one situated in the midlands. One of the ten randomly identified schools was a girls' grammar school, one was a girls' comprehensive school and the remaining eight were mixed comprehensives. Schools already identified as including contemporary art practice were removed from the sampling frame for this randomly selected group. This cohort will be referred to throughout the report as the randomly identified schools.

The sample of eight schools identified as actively incorporating contemporary art practice within their curriculum at key stage 3 and 4 were purposively selected through information provided by Tate, ACE, local gallery education officers and a local art adviser. The definition of what constituted contemporary art practice, or of a school that demonstrated a commitment to this, was left entirely to those identifying the schools. Thus, schools in this sample did not necessarily approach the art curriculum in the same way or incorporate contemporary art practice to the same degree. Conversely, schools in the randomly identified sample did not necessarily omit contemporary art practice from their curriculum; they were simply not identified to the researchers as schools that actively included it. From the list provided, the sample of CAP identified schools was selected to represent a geographical spread and included three schools in the north of England and two from the south (including one in London). The three schools selected for extended visits comprised one in north-east England, one in a rural part of the south west and one in central London.

In all of the sample schools interviews were carried out with the head of the art department and with a number of their colleagues, depending on the size of the department. All interviewees were asked about:

- their own professional background
- the content of the art curriculum they delivered
- factors affecting their choice of curriculum content
- their perceptions of the impacts and learning outcomes of the art curriculum as taught.

In addition, heads of department were asked about the contents and foci of the key stage 3 and 4 art curricula in general in their school and for a curriculum overview. Relevant documentation was collected as available. A section of each interview with both heads of department and art teachers was specific to a given year group, to gain a more detailed picture of the content of the art curriculum for that year. It was not possible to conduct interviews that covered all of the year groups in each key stage in all schools, therefore year groups were purposely selected to ensure an even spread of data and an average of 12 interviews per year group was achieved, with an average of three year groups covered in each department. In addition, data collection in the three schools receiving an extended visit was widened to include pupil interviews and lesson observations, which allowed for some limited triangulation of the views expressed, particularly concerning the perceived outcomes and impacts of contemporary art programmes.

Most of the art teachers were also asked to respond to a sample of six images, depicting art works from a range of artists including Van Gogh, David Shrigley and Damien Hirst (see Chapter 3 for more details) as a way of further understanding their selection of curriculum content. For the most part, heads of department were not asked to respond to these images because of the additional demand that the research process made on their time.

Additional emphasis was placed on the inclusion of contemporary art practice in interviews with teachers in the CAP identified sample of schools.

The interview schedules, which were designed to address the objectives of the project as set out earlier in the text, were piloted in three schools not included in the main samples and subsequently revised in the light of this piloting.

1.2.4 Interviewees in the sample

A total of 54 teachers (including 18 heads of departments) were interviewed from the 18 schools (an average of three teachers per school). Of these, two were student teachers, one interviewee was a newly qualified teacher and one interviewee was an American exchange teacher. (It was recognised that these members of staff would not always be aware of the ethos and direction of the department to the same degree as their full time or more established colleagues, but that their views would still be valid in establishing a picture of the curriculum as taught.) The heads of department interviewed ranged in experience; four interviewees had been appointed in the past three years, and six had been in post for over 20 years.

Details concerning the professional background of interviewees in the sample are addressed in Chapter 3. In addition to their background as artists, the interviewees were asked whether or not they viewed themselves as practising artists at the time of interview. There was a general consensus that, despite a desire to continue working as an artist, the pressures of teaching left the interviewees with little time to explore this, particularly for full-time members of staff and those with young children. A number of interviewees commented that the majority of their energy and artistic creativity went into helping their pupils achieve.

> *I find that when I'm busy, my own work is the thing that takes a back burner; you give everything to the kids really, your ideas and your creativity.*
> Head of department, randomly identified school

Naturally, those teachers employed in school part time felt they had more time and more opportunities to develop their own practice and it was mainly those interviewees that were able to talk about currently exhibiting and selling their work.

Despite these time constraints it was recognised that maintaining an interest in producing art, outside of school, was beneficial for teachers wishing to continually develop their areas of expertise and interest and was also beneficial for the pupils.

I think it is important to sometimes let the children see that you are a practising person.
Art teacher, randomly identified school

1.2.5 Analysis

All interviews were recorded and extensive summaries were made of each interview. These summaries were entered into MAXQDA. Interviews were coded so that all data could be retrieved and sorted according to school type (CAP or randomly identified), interviewee role and year group covered. Answers to each of the questions could be separately retrieved for analysis. Some parts of the data lent themselves to rudimentary quantitative analysis, while for others a qualitative analysis of interviewees' accounts was more appropriate. Where possible, both approaches have been combined to give an understanding of the number of responses of particular types, and a sense of the specific views being expressed. It is readily acknowledged that the sample size for this research was not large, however, the data is rich and in many respects detailed, and while not presuming to be representative, it is presented in a way that is intended to be both indicative and illustrative.

1.3 The structure of the report

The report begins by setting out an overview of the content and foci of the school art curriculum as taught at key stage 3 and 4. Chapter 2 documents the following:

- skills taught
- formal elements addressed
- media and materials used
- thinking processes demanded of students
- cultural references deployed by teachers to support the curriculum.

This chapter also explores the status and nature of contemporary art practice within school art and the extent to which it is evident as a part of the curriculum.

Chapter 3 considers factors that influence the choice of curriculum content, paying particular attention to how these affect the inclusion of contemporary art practice. As well as their responses to specific questions, teachers were invited to respond to a selection of images and their appropriateness for inclusion as curriculum references.

Chapter 4 discusses the perceived benefits of programmes incorporating contemporary art practice from the teacher's perspective, with limited reference to pupil perspectives.

The report concludes in Chapter 5 by summarising a series of questions raised by the research findings and a discussion of the possible strategies for further addressing the future development of the art curriculum.

Appendix 1 contains the report of the literature review.

2 The content of the art curriculum in secondary schools

2.1 Introduction

This chapter discusses the structure of the school art curriculum at key stage 3 and 4, underlying curriculum design principles and the sample of art modules as described by interviewees (see section 2.2).

Section 2.3 goes on to explore the salient contents and foci of school art by looking in detail at the following elements of 'content':

- the use of media or materials
- the artistic and cultural references used to support teaching and learning
- the skills taught, including the formal elements of art addressed
- the thinking processes developed through, or used to support, the study of art.

These are gleaned from interviewees' descriptions of 62 art modules.

Section 2.4 explores other aspects of curriculum content, including the use of external resources, issues as raised in art modules and links with other curriculum areas, again extracted primarily from interviewees' descriptions of art modules.

By identifying aspects of the curriculum that featured more prevalently in the modules described by teachers in CAP identified schools, a range of characteristics that might be associated with contemporary art practice in schools emerged. These characteristics are based on grounded research and empirical evidence rather than on pre-determined definitions of contemporary art practice. These characteristics are discussed in section 2.5.

The chapter concludes with a summary (section 2.6).

2.2 The structure of the school art curriculum at key stage 3 and 4

Interviewees were asked how the art curriculum they taught was structured throughout key stage 3 and 4, and then specifically about the structure of the curriculum for the particular year group that featured in their own interview. It emerged that there was consensus between staff within each department concerning their overall curriculum structure and design. The interview data was supported in most cases by departmental documents. Analysis was therefore undertaken at school rather than teacher level, based on department documents and head of department interviews.

2.2.1 Underlying curriculum design principles

Art departments were invited to supply course documentation that might further inform the research process. Heads of departments were also asked to describe their overall approach to the curriculum through years 7–11.

The paperwork provided by departments was uneven in both amount and content and, given the considerable demands being made on schools taking part in the research, researchers were content to accept what the schools chose to supply. For the most part, documents relating to the department as a whole tended to address structural issues, supplying information that was required for monitoring and inspection purposes, and setting out the basic requirements and structure of what needed to be covered. Most schools also provided a sample of module plans. These identified the skills to be taught, the materials to be used and in some cases, referred to artists that might be referred to in the teaching process. Most schools also identified generic learning areas to be addressed, for example, literacy and IT skills. While the majority provided a general outline for teachers to follow, in one case a teacher provided a highly specific plan, based on her own interests and engagement with a particular work of art.

Only three of the sample schools provided documentation that went considerably beyond this somewhat utilitarian approach, offering documentation that expressed a philosophical standpoint in relation to both art and art teaching. One of them included policy statements concerning, for example, 'equal opportunities, art and gender', 'art and culture' and 'spiritual, moral, social and cultural'. Another school provided a policy document setting out its understanding of the purpose of art teaching, perhaps characterised by the following statement.

> *The intention is to provide a creative education rather than carry on a programme of 'doing art'.*
> Policy document, CAP identified school

The document went on to describe art as 'a magnificent teaching vehicle' and clearly expressed the intention to relate learning in art to other areas of the curriculum.

This is not to suggest that those schools that did not supply such documentation lacked a philosophical standpoint, or even lacked documentation describing it. It may be that they simply did not choose to make such material available to the researchers.

A similarly wide range of responses met the interview question 'Could you describe your overall approach to the curriculum through years 7–11?'. The use of the term 'approach' permitted interviewees to choose to respond with either a structural or a philosophical slant. The following range of foci for their descriptions emerged from the answers given by the heads of department in the 18 schools (eight CAP and ten randomly identified). Interviewees cited up to four different points in describing their overall approaches (numbers indicate the number of teachers in each cohort of schools referring to each point).

- The structural approach, involving the description of pupil groupings, modular structures, and so on (randomly identified schools =6, CAP identified schools =1).

- A description of teaching and learning as a progression, initially focusing on the directed development of skills (primarily art-making skills) and moving towards a more exploratory approach, experimenting with media and ideas (randomly identified schools =8, CAP identified schools =8).

- An approach that accentuated pupil response or experience, including the generation of a sense of achievement (or avoidance of failure), fun and the encouragement of inspiration and interest (randomly identified schools =3, CAP identified schools =5).

- An emphasis of the intention that teachers devise teaching programmes to suit their own skills and experience (randomly identified schools =2, CAP identified schools =3).

- The incorporation of new ideas, current events and other stimuli into the curriculum, such as gallery exhibitions (randomly identified schools =0, CAP identified schools =3).

Again, it is important to recognise that even if interviewees did not make references to each of the approaches as set out above, this does not mean that such approaches did not apply, only that they did not choose to mention them.

From the above it can be seen that 16 of the 18 heads of department referred to a commitment to the teaching of art skills, particularly at the start of the secondary curriculum. All 16 indicated that they followed a progression throughout the key stages, starting with a basic introduction to skills, techniques and a range of media in year 7 and gradually building and expanding on this throughout key stage 3. By key stage 4, interviewees felt that pupils should have sufficient basic skills to begin to work in a more exploratory way, bringing in more artist references and experimenting with both media and ideas. This exploratory working was frequently linked to more independent learning. Thus, it was an apparently orthodox view that the teaching of art form skills needed to precede experimentation and the generation of ideas. This understanding of the overall curriculum design was shared by the vast majority of the 54 teachers interviewed.

> *I think very much that in key stage 3, the pupil should have a good grounding in the fundamentals of art and I have a real belief in teaching skills … giving them skills so that they can become independent learners, so that once they have settled into year 10 they can take more responsibility for their own learning,* [and become] *more independent, more individual.*
> Art teacher, randomly identified school

Year 9 stood out within this overall curriculum approach; as the year before GCSE it was often seen as an opportunity to 'sell' the GCSE course to those pupils who had yet to choose their options. Pupils in year 9 were also encouraged to begin working in a GCSE format through the introduction of sketch books, design sheets and project-based work as preparation for those individuals intending to study art. Thus, in the majority of schools the emphasis of the art curriculum began to shift away from being primarily skills-based to the introduction of more exploratory art work in year 9.

> *We try in year 9 to build up an understanding of how an art project works – ready to start GCSE*
> Head of department, CAP identified school

A smaller number of heads of department (eight) referred to a pupil-centred pedagogical approach, which provided opportunities for pupils of all abilities to succeed, regardless of apparent 'artistic talent'. For example, in one case, the interviewee discussed the ethos of the department and his/her desire to provide a curriculum in which all pupils could achieve, by including opportunities for exploratory work and avoiding too much emphasis on skill.

> *We purposefully avoid putting up barriers which lead to failure – we need to get rid of the notion that they* [the pupils] *can or can't draw.*
> Head of department, CAP identified school

> *We try and make it as broad and accessible to as many pupils as possible. We try and enable every pupil to achieve, so in our schemes of work we try and differentiate as much as possible so that the lower ability are always able to achieve and the higher abilities are able to work more independently.*
> Head of department, CAP identified school

Five heads of department highlighted the principle that teachers within their departments devise teaching programmes to suit their own skills and experience, primarily by adapting or devising schemes of work so that they reflected their own strengths in terms of media, materials and artistic references. (See section 2.2.2 below for more information on how schemes of work were devised.)

Three heads of department, all from CAP identified schools, highlighted their commitment to providing a broad and inclusive curriculum and focused their answer on the inclusion of contemporary art practice within their departments. In all three cases, providing a broad and inclusive range of curriculum references was seen as an enhancement to, rather than replacement of, a curriculum based on a skills-led progression. For example, a module on natural forms was taught in year 7 to encourage good observational drawing skills, which were valued highly by the interviewee. However, contemporary artists such as Anish Kapoor, various fashion designers and a large installation in Soho Square were all used as references and were seen as making the teaching of traditional skills and techniques 'more interesting'.

From such an open-ended question, it is understandable that responses should be so varied. However, it is perhaps surprising that so few interviewees chose to interpret the word 'approach' in the question as meaning philosophical approach, or approach to the purpose and meaning of the art and of art teaching. Few chose to talk 'outside the box' of structures, patterns and progression.

In conclusion, two distinct approaches have emerged from the analysis of the way in which teachers discussed the structure of the art curriculum in the sample schools. The prevalent response was reference to a directed, skills-orientated approach, moving towards a more exploratory approach, experimenting with media and ideas, frequently linked to more independent learning. In a smaller proportion of schools this was accompanied by an approach that was more teacher and pupil centred, paying particular attention to creating opportunities for achievement and enjoyment and allowing for teachers' own skills and experiences to influence the curriculum content. In three CAP identified schools the curriculum approach was also described as inclusive, providing opportunities for gallery visits and the incorporation of new ideas and current events.

The overall curriculum design for the two key stages emerged as distinct, but related, in all schools.

2.2.2 Differentiation of the key stages

Key stage 3

The overall aim of the National Curriculum key stage 3 programme of study for art and design is that:

> *Teaching should ensure that investigating and making includes exploring and developing ideas, and evaluating and developing work. Knowledge and understanding should inform this process.*
> QCA (2003c, p.1)

The QCA provides schemes of work that suggest specific artists, topics and skills. However, the actual curriculum content selected to achieve these objectives is at the discretion of the individual art department or teacher. The use of the QCA schemes of work is not mandatory. Indeed, it is explicitly stated in the QCA documentation that schools are free to devise their own ways of meeting the requirements of the National Curriculum. In addition, it is stated that teachers should select from, and customise the schemes of work, so that the curriculum they provide is better suited to the school and to the pupils' needs and abilities (QCA, 2004).

The majority of the art departments in the sample divided their key stage 3 curriculum into modules or projects (three projects per year in 14 of the 18 schools) with headings that at least resembled those suggested by the QCA. For example, interviewees frequently made reference to units of work on landscape, natural forms, objects and viewpoints, identity and portraiture, all of which are themes suggested in the QCA schemes of work. However, when asked if they followed the content of the QCA schemes of work, only one department stated this was the case, choosing to do so because of the 'intellectual stimulation' they felt the QCA schemes provided for their pupils.

Three further approaches to devising schemes of work emerged.

- Modified departmental QCA schemes of work were used by teachers in seven departments (five in randomly identified schools and two in CAP identified schools). These schemes of work were based on the QCA proposed schemes, or more specifically on their themes and headings (as discussed earlier), but changed and adapted to suit the needs of pupils and individual teachers' particular interest and skills. The majority felt that the QCA schemes, as written, were too difficult for their pupils in terms of manageability within a given time frame.

- Departmentally devised schemes of work were used in eight schools (four in CAP identified schools and four in randomly identified schools). Interviewees in these schools had devised their own units of work as a department, or individual teachers had contributed to a central store. In all cases these centrally held schemes of work were open for adaptation by individual teachers as long as the overall objectives were covered. Whilst these schemes were not necessarily adapted from the QCA proposed schemes, they did show a number of similarities, particularly with the themes covered.

- Individually devised schemes were used in two departments (one in a randomly identified school and one in a CAP identified school). In these schools individual teachers wrote their own schemes of work under central themes for each year group. There was no reference to the sharing of these schemes with other members of the department and no reference to the use of QCA or other existing schemes.

The above approaches were frequently perceived as a way of allowing new ideas, developments in the wider art world and current exhibitions to be incorporated into the curriculum, and to avoid teaching becoming restricted or 'stale'.

It puts teachers in the situation where they have to be creative.
Head of department, randomly identified school

No reference was made to commercially available schemes of work.

Key stage 4

All of the schools in the research sample offered a GCSE course in Art at key stage 4. Eleven of the 18 departments followed the Assessment and Qualifications Alliance (AQA) unendorsed syllabus and six had selected the EdExcel unendorsed syllabus. One school offered the AQA endorsed course, where pupils selected a specialist media in which the majority of their coursework must be presented. This was resisted by the majority because they either felt their department did not have the resources, human or other, to be able to offer specialisms, or they preferred to provide a curriculum that offered breadth as opposed to depth. Conversely, the school that did follow the endorsed course chose to do so because of the opportunity it provided for working in depth.

> *We don't see any point in students doing a bit of this and a bit of that, because then they never get really good at anything. By working on a specialism they can develop and get stronger and stronger so by the controlled test in year 11 they have the confidence and skills to do something really good.*
> Teacher, CAP identified school

However, an unendorsed course was also offered as an option in this school for pupils who did not suit the endorsed course.

Other reasons given for syllabus selection included departmental tradition, a preference for a particular marking structure (including perceptions of a fairer moderating system) and a past history of good results with a particular exam board.

> *When I came to work here, I inherited students that were half way through the AQA syllabus. So we stayed with it for the year and we achieved very good GCSE results. So we stuck with it.*
> Head of department, randomly identified school

In conclusion, the data suggests that the individual art departments, and in most cases the individual teacher, had considerable control over the content of the art curriculum taught in secondary schools. This individualisation of content may be greater than in other curriculum areas, and may indicate the need to be aware of the motivations and attitudes of art teachers, if the curriculum as taught is to be understood.

2.3 The content of art modules and schemes of work, as delivered by secondary school art teachers

Analysis of curriculum content is based primarily on the data collected in the section of each interview that focused on a particular module, project or scheme of work for a particular year group. Because modules were discussed from a range of year groups (in key stage 3 and 4) and across the whole academic year, collectively they may be seen as reasonably indicative of the curriculum taught.

However, it is fully accepted that this is a limited sample.

A total of 34 modules were discussed by teachers in the ten randomly selected schools. The 28 modules described in the eight CAP identified schools have been analysed as a distinct data set, in order to ascertain any characteristics that may distinguish them from the more 'typical' curriculum. Where data from both cohorts are included in a unit of analysis, this is indicated.

In reporting the findings, frequencies are often relayed as percentages as well as numbers in order to illustrate the difference between the two cohorts of schools. Because of the sample size, the differences between actual numbers may sometimes be very small and findings should therefore be seen as indicative rather than representative.

This section is descriptive and provides an overall picture of the content of school art lessons. The reasons underpinning the decisions made by teachers, which lead to the selection of content as outlined below, are discussed in Chapter 3.

The content of modules is divided into the following subsections:

- the media and materials used
- the artistic and cultural references deployed
- the skills taught and the formal terms of art addressed
- the thinking processes developed by, or demanded of pupils.

2.3.1 The use of media and materials

Interviewees were asked to list the media and materials that pupils were encouraged to work with in the course of the module under consideration. There is evidence of pupil choice concerning the use of media and materials in just under a quarter of the 34 modules in the randomly identified schools. The percentage was slightly higher in the modules in the CAP identified schools with two fifths of interviewees in this cohort identifying pupil choice in the use of media and materials.

Interviewees accounts of the media and materials used in the modules have been classified into several categories.

- **Painting and drawing:** paint, pencil, pen and ink, charcoal, crayon and so on, used for creating two-dimensional (2D) images and for the development of the skills associated with the manipulation of these 'basic' art materials.

- **Three-dimensional (3D) Materials:**
    - clay, thumb pots
    - found objects, including litter and drift wood, which was then used to create art works
    - other 3D materials such as card, modrock, chicken wire and so on.
- **Collage:** using textured paper, fabric, string etc
- **Textiles:** weaving, quilting, batik or fabric painting featured in some of the modules discussed. In one example pupils produced weavings based on the landscape imagery of the post-impressionists and on their own initial sketches
- **Printing:** including linocuts, mono-printing and screen-printing. One example of the use of printing was the development of a portrait module in which students produced lino cuts of their original drawings to explore the effective use of line and mark making
- **ICT:** examples of the use of ICT primarily focused on the use of Photoshop and other digital image manipulation software, often introduced towards the end of a scheme of work for pupils to further develop their existing painted or drawn images. More examples of the use of ICT are discussed in section 2.5
- **Other:** which included sand, chamois, newspaper clippings, expandable foam and rubber, often used in a exploratory way by pupils themselves to create a desired effect, rather than being instructed by teachers.

Figure 2.1 shows the range of media and materials used in both the modules in the randomly identified schools and the modules in the CAP identified schools.

The data for the modules in the randomly identified schools gives an indication of the general picture concerning the use of media and materials in school art.

- The most commonly used media in the modules was painting and drawing, featuring in 29 (85 per cent) of the modules described. Collectively, 3D materials, including the subcategories of clay, found objects and other materials, featured as the second most popular category in 19 (56 per cent) of the modules in randomly identified schools.
- ICT as a medium for creating art does not feature in any of the modules in the randomly identified schools, although it was frequently mentioned by teachers as a resource for researching artists and art works, predominantly through the use of the internet.

- Photography, as a medium used by pupils, was noticeable by its absence from the modules in both CAP and the randomly identified schools, as was the moving image (although in one CAP identified school there was reference to the opportunity to work in film). Photographs were referred to as sources for observational drawing and to document pupils' work, but not as a medium for creating art. However, photography was included as an art form in the references used to support the curriculum (see section 2.3.2).

Figure 2.1 Media and materials used

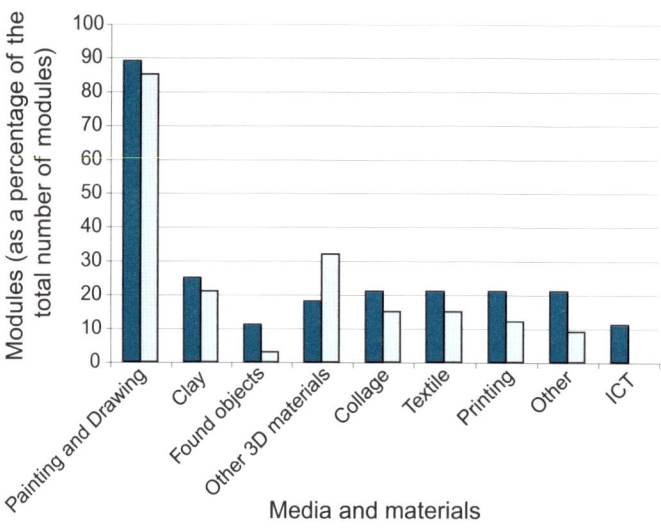

■ Modules in CAP identified schools, □ Modules in randomly identified schools
N = 62 modules. A number of modules incorporated more than one medium, thus the categories are not mutually exclusive.
Source: NFER interviews conducted with art teachers and heads of art departments (2003/2004)

None of the modules described included the moving image as a medium for art making, although one teacher referred to opportunities existing within the department and another regretted its absence.

The figures shown in Figure 2.1 demonstrate the range of the media and materials being used across both key stage 3 and 4 in the randomly selected schools. When the data is considered by key stage the following observations can be made.

- The most common category featured in modules at both key stages was painting and drawing. However, this featured in a lower proportion of key stage 4 modules (67 per cent) compared to key stage 3 modules (95 per cent).

- At key stage 4, 3D materials, including clay, found objects and other, were used in ten modules, and painting and drawing featured in eight. At key stage 3, ten modules incorporated 3D materials and 21 used painting and drawing. This perhaps indicates a more balanced use of 2D and 3D materials at key stage 4 than at key stage 3.
- Found objects only feature in descriptions of key stage 4 modules.

Differences between modules in CAP and randomly identified schools

When the media and materials used in the randomly identified schools are compared with those specified in the CAP identified school modules, regular patterns can be discerned.

- 2D materials remains the highest ranking category, used in 89 per cent of the modules in the CAP identified schools (compared to 85 per cent of modules in the randomly identified schools).
- 3D materials, including clay, found objects and other materials, featured in just over half of the modules in both CAP and randomly identified schools.
- The subcategory of found objects featured in two modules in the CAP identified schools and one module in a randomly identified school.
- The categories of collage, textiles and printing all featured more prevalently in the modules in the CAP identified schools.
- ICT, as an art creating medium, only featured in modules in the CAP identified schools.

The media and materials used in the curriculum can be seen as indicative of the shift from a predominantly skills-led approach in key stage 3 (primarily the development of painting and drawing skills), to the inclusion of more exploratory media at key stage 4, which may indicate a progression from skills to more experimental approaches. Analysis of the media used in the CAP identified schools suggests a curriculum similar to that provided in the randomly identified schools in the use of traditional 2D and 3D materials. The modules in CAP identified schools appear to allow for more exploration of ICT and other more experimental materials (found objects, collage, textiles, printing and so on). However, it is important to acknowledge that these variations in the use of media and materials between modules in the CAP and randomly identified schools are, in general, only marginal.

2.3.2 The artistic and cultural references included in the curriculum

Interviewees were questioned about the artistic and cultural references they used to support the modules they were describing. The question was posed 'Did the students study any particular artists in this module?' and this resulted in an extensive list of artists, genres and art forms.

Artists and genres

For analysis purposes these have been grouped together under the various historical periods/headings.

- **Art pre 1800:** including Medieval and Renaissance.
- **19th century European Art:** primarily Romanticism, Realism and Impressionism.
- **Early 20th century and abstract art:** including Fauvism, Expressionism and Cubism.
- **Art between the wars in Europe:** primarily Dada and Surrealism.
- **Mid-20th-century art:** including Abstract Expressionism, pop art and Minimalism.
- **Art in the latter 20th and early 21st century:** including conceptual and installation art and any art produced from 1970 to the present day.
- International art/culture: from all time periods (although references used in this category were almost entirely from the earlier historical periods).

A further category of **'other'** was included, covering unnamed artists, local artists known to the school (in one case a relative of the art teacher) or examples where the work of a teacher or another pupil was the reference.

Figure 2.2 shows the range of art movements referred to in the modules in both the CAP and randomly identified schools. In the figure, the number of modules reporting particular features have been shown as percentages in order to illustrate comparisons between CAP and randomly identified schools. However, it should be stressed that the actual numbers upon which the percentages are based are frequently very low.

Analysis of the modules in the randomly identified schools revealed the following information.

- In just over two-fifths (41 per cent) of the modules described, teachers referred to images, artists or genres associated with the early 20th century in Europe to support the curriculum.

- The second most common historical time periods used as references to support the curriculum emerged as the 19th century and mid-20th century, again focusing on European art movements (work from each of these periods was used in 18 per cent of the modules in the randomly identified schools).

- No references were made to international art/culture in the modules in the randomly identified schools.

- Very few references (less than 10 per cent) were made to art pre-1800 or art between the wars in Europe.

Figure 2.2 Artists used as references to support the curriculum, identified by period

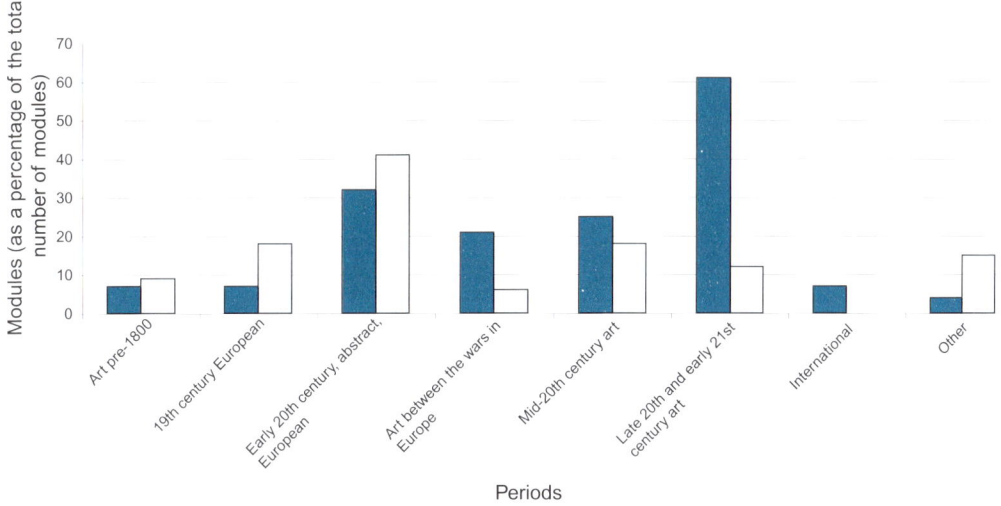

■ Modules in CAP identified schools, □ Modules in randomly identified schools
N = 62 modules. A number of modules incorporated references from more than one time period, thus the categories are not mutually exclusive.
Source: NFER interviews conducted with art teachers and heads of art departments (2003/2004)

The three frequently cited historical periods (early 20th century in Europe, 19th century European and mid-20th century) appeared to have been selected because of their accessibility for the pupils. The skills represented in the images were perceived as important for the students to learn and ones that pupils of all abilities could identify and develop in their own work. Again, this was indicative of a skills-orientated approach to curriculum design.

> *He [Gustav Klimt] is accessible to the students. The shapes he uses are easy to copy and are familiar to the pupils – triangles, eyes etc. The colours, the golds and silvers are pleasing and the pupils tend to like his work.*
> Art teacher, randomly identified school

The factors affecting the artistic references chosen by teachers are explored in more depth in Chapter 3.

The figures given in Figure 2.2 show the artistic and cultural references used across both key stage 3 and 4 in the randomly selected schools. The following findings emerged from analysis of the data by key stage.

- Artists and works of art pre-1800, or art between the wars in Europe was referred to in key stage 3 modules only.
- Early 20th century and abstract art in Europe featured in 55 per cent of key stage 4 modules compared to 17 per cent of key stage 3 modules.

In five key stage 4 modules in the randomly identified schools, interviewees commented that the pupils were allowed to select the artistic references themselves. This was not the case in any key stage 3 modules in the randomly identified schools. Therefore these findings may be to some extent indicative of pupil preference concerning artists and art movements, as well as of teacher choice. Where pupil choice was indicated by interviewees, there was again recognition that images were selected because of their perceived accessibility.

> *Most of them [the pupils] chose artists they liked and which they thought they could use. The impressionists were popular, I think because the techniques are accessible.*
> Head of department, randomly identified school

Differences between modules in CAP and randomly identified schools

When the cultural and artistic references used in the modules in the randomly identified schools are compared with those in the CAP identified schools, regular patterns can be discerned.

- The most popular historical period from which artistic and cultural references were selected in the CAP identified schools was Art in the latter 20th and early 21st century. References from this period were used in 61 per cent of the modules in the CAP identified schools compared to just 12 per cent of the modules in the randomly identified schools.

- Nineteenth century European art was three times as likely to have featured in randomly identified schools than in CAP identified schools (18 per cent compared to 6 per cent), though it is important to note the low actual numbers involved (6 and 2).

- International art/culture featured only in the modules as described in the CAP identified schools. Its inclusion predominantly consisted of historical cultural references such as Islamic pattern, Egyptian hieroglyphics and Aboriginal art, rather than the work of individual or contemporary artists (although in one case the teacher had found a book of images by a single contemporary Aboriginal artist).

Artists by gender and nationality

The artists included were analysed by nationality and gender. As indicated by the categories mentioned earlier, the majority of the art movements referred to originated in Europe and were led by predominantly European artists. American artists were primarily from the pop art movement and genres associated with the latter 20th and early 21st century. Other than the international art/culture already discussed above, there was only one reference to an artist of any other nationality, Anna Bella Geiger, a Brazilian photographer and printmaker working in the latter 20th century.

Out of a total of 72 interviewees, only eight of the artists mentioned were women. Of these eight, five were producing art in the latter 20th century. Overall, this may be regarded as a considerable under-representation of women artists, but may also reflect their growing influence in the art world in the latter 20th century. Six of the eight female artists were referred to in modules in the CAP identified schools only, with Georgia O'Keefe and Bridget Reilly being the only women artists referred to in modules from the randomly identified schools.

2.3.3 Art forms

It emerged that the artistic references used to support the curriculum represented a range of art forms. For analysis purposes, the artists referred to by the teachers were categorised by the media in which they primarily worked, or for which their work is most well known (on the assumption that this would be the art form in which pupils would have been exposed to their work).

Figure 2.3 shows the range of art forms referred to in modules in both the CAP and the randomly identified schools.

Figure 2.3 Art forms used as references to support the curriculum

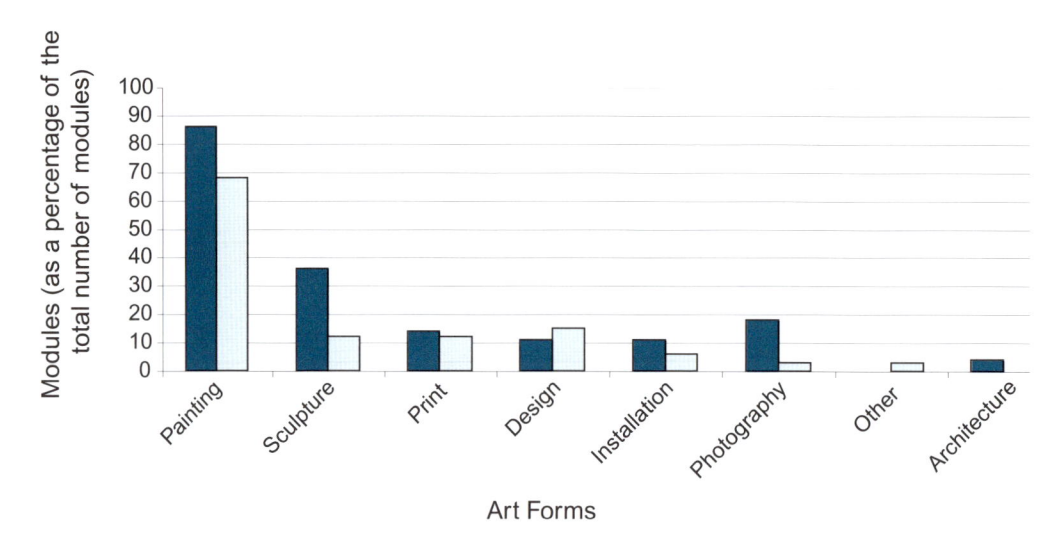

■ Modules in CAP identified schools, □ Modules in randomly identified schools
N = 62 modules. A number of modules referred to more than one art form, thus the categories are not mutually exclusive.
Source: NFER interviews conducted with art teachers and heads of art departments (2003/2004).

Analysis of the modules in the randomly identified schools revealed that the artistic references used were primarily in the form of paintings, followed by design (such as poster design and textile design) and print. This is perhaps because 2D art was often perceived by the interviewees as more manageable for use in the classroom. Normally, 2D images are more readily available, in books, as posters and postcards and on the internet. In addition, 2D images can easily be stored and looked at in the classroom setting (in two schools teachers referred to the use of whiteboards to show a series of artistic images to pupils). To really appreciate 3D art often requires that it is seen 'in the flesh', sometimes literally. This opinion was highlighted by two teachers' reluctance to use a photograph of Damien Hirst's *The physical impossibility of death in the mind of someone living*, as a reference in the classroom, because a flat image of this piece would not allow students to fully understand its impact (see Chapter 3 for more details). Art forms other than painting each featured in less than 20 per cent of the modules in the randomly identified schools. Although the moving image was not screened in any module as a reference, two teachers referred to film, in one case to describe the use of light and in another to refer to the film design work of an artist (Geiger).

Analysis of the art forms that made up the references chosen by teachers across the key stages shows that painting remained the most frequently cited art form across both key stages. Examples of paintings were referred to in 73 per cent of key stage 3 modules and 58 per cent of key stage 4 modules. Print and design each featured in a quarter (25 per cent) of the key stage 4 modules compared to less than 10 per cent of the key stage 3 modules, suggesting less reliance on painting at key stage 4 but not necessarily more inclusion of 3D references.

Differences between modules in CAP and randomly identified schools

There were some variations between the citation of particular art forms in the modules in the CAP identified schools and the modules in the randomly identified.

- Photography featured in five (18 per cent) of modules in the CAP identified schools compared to just one (3 per cent) module in a randomly identified school.

- Sculpture was referred to in 36 per cent of modules in the CAP identified schools compared to 12 per cent of modules in the randomly identified schools.

- Architecture was used in one CAP identified school module but not in the randomly identified schools.

The modules in the randomly identified schools included references to an average of one historical art period, and included works of art in an average of one art form (predominantly painting). The modules in the CAP identified schools included references to an average of two historical art periods and pupils were exposed to an average of two different art forms. Thus, the CAP identified schools provided twice as many artistic references to support the curriculum as the randomly identified schools. Whether an engagement with contemporary art practice leads to a wider menu of artistic reference, or vice versa, is not apparent from the data. Irrespective of the presence, or absence, of a causal connection, schools that were identified as engaging with contemporary art practice have emerged in the data as also drawing on a much larger range and volume of art references.

2.3.4 The skills taught, including the formal elements of art addressed

Interviewees were asked to identify the main skills being taught through the modules under discussion. In the majority of cases, this included references to the formal elements of art.

The skills taught were classified into groups.

- **Manipulation of materials:** art form skills including applying paint, working with clay and developing specific techniques such as cross hatching, collage and lino printing.
- **Formal elements:** space, line, tone, colour and texture.
- **Research skills:** researching artists, genres and researching topics as stimuli for work. This was frequently supported through the use of the internet and was often set as homework to accompany the module.
- **Observational drawing:** from both primary and secondary sources.
- **Using art to express meaning:** the use of colour and the other formal elements to express mood and create atmosphere, telling a story through composition or making a statement about a particular issue through a piece of art. For example, one module focused on how colour and tone can be used in portraits to indicate the mood of the subject. In another module pupils were asked to create a narrative that involved themselves and elements of contemporary society (such as themselves appearing in a current movie or talking on a mobile phone) and then build up a picture around this narrative.

Figure 2.4 shows the range of skills taught in both the modules in the randomly identified schools and the modules in the CAP identified schools.

Analysis of the modules in the randomly identified schools revealed the following.

- Each of the formal elements (space, line, tone, colour and texture) was addressed in approximately a quarter of the modules in the randomly identified schools, but 32 per cent of the modules in the randomly identified schools made no reference to formal elements.
- Observational drawing featured as a specific skill taught in 13 (38 per cent) of the modules in the randomly identified schools and was frequently highlighted as a valuable skill.

We do value, very highly, the use of observational drawing as a starting point – not to intimidate those who can't draw, but as a way of really engaging with your environment – looking, seeing and engaging with what you are seeing.
Head of department, randomly identified school

- It is noticeable that both research skills and teaching pupils to express meaning, ranked significantly lower than the other three categories. This suggested a tendency to concentrate on the craft skills of art making rather than on critical and expressive skills.

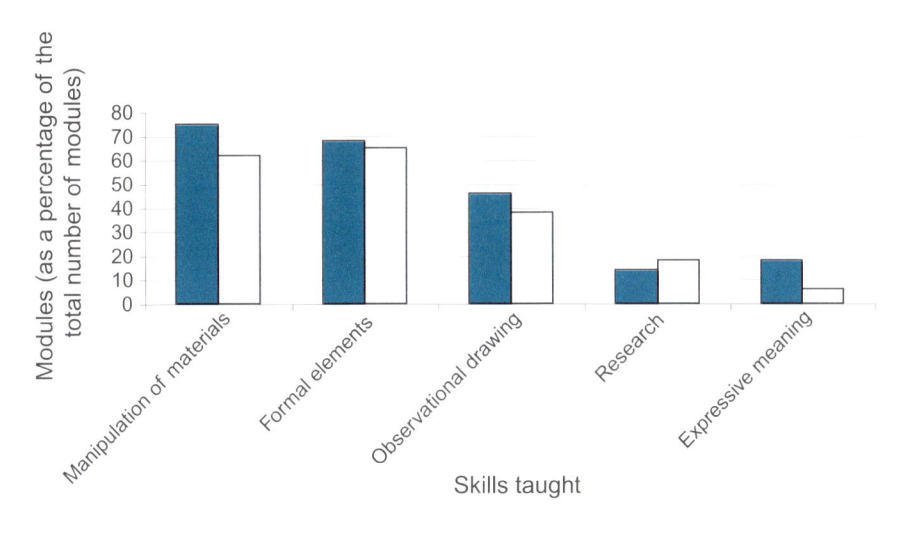

Figure 2.4 The skills taught

■ Modules in CAP identified schools, □ Modules in randomly identified schools
N = 62 modules. A number of interviewees referred to more than one skill, thus the categories are not mutually exclusive.
Source: NFER interviews conducted with art teachers and heads of art departments (2003/2004).

The figures given in figure 2.4 show the range of skills being taught across key stage 3 and 4 in the randomly selected schools. When the two key stages are looked at individually the order of frequency in which the skills are ranked remains the same. Research skills, however, were taught in just 10 per cent of key stage 3 modules compared to 27 per cent of key stage 4 modules. The assessment criteria for GCSE emphasises the need for students to carry out research, which may account for this differentiation, but this raises the question as to why research was not highlighted as a feature of all the key stage 4 modules. It is possible that research is so fundamental to the work that is being done, particularly at GCSE level, that interviewees did not identify it as a separate skill. It is also possible that research was often done as homework, or not under direct teacher supervision, so that whilst research was taking place, research skills were not actually being taught.

Differences between modules in CAP and randomly identified schools

When the skills taught in the modules in the randomly identified schools are compared with those identified in the CAP identified schools, the order of frequency remains the same. The only significant difference being expression of meaning, referred to as being taught as a skill area in 18 per cent of modules in the CAP identified schools compared to 6 per cent of modules in the randomly identified schools. The ways in which this skill was taught in the CAP identified schools is explored in more detail in section 2.5.

2.3.5 The thinking processes developed by, or demanded of pupils

Interviewees were asked to comment on the thinking processes their students used to support the work done in each module. They were also asked how students generated their ideas and to what extent analysis and evaluation featured in the curriculum.

The answers given to these three questions were then classified.

- **Analysing and evaluating:** this sub-divided as follows:
    - pupils analysing and evaluating artists
    - analysing and evaluating their classmates and peers work
    - analysing and evaluating their own work.
- **Creating and making:** choosing appropriate materials and techniques, making compositional decisions and the progressive development of ideas (often through the use of sketch books and design sheets, particularly at key stage 4 where a record of the development of ideas needs to be shown for assessment purposes).
- **Investigation/research:** as a process that the students were expected to undertake as part of the process of creating an art work, differentiated from research as a taught skill since responses included unsupervised research or investigative tasks set as homework.
- **Creative thinking processes:** giving personal responses, experimenting with both materials and ideas and thinking conceptually.

Figure 2.5 shows the thinking processes developed in the modules in the randomly identified schools compared to the modules in the CAP identified schools.

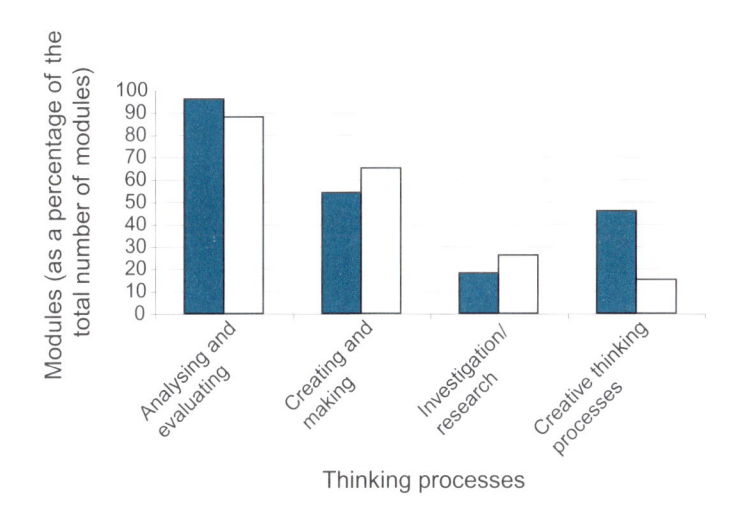

Figure 2.5 The thinking processes used in, and developed through the modules

```
Modules (as a percentage of the total number of modules)
100
 90
 80
 70
 60
 50
 40
 30
 20
 10
  0
     Analysing and   Creating and   Investigation/   Creative thinking
      evaluating       making          research         processes
                        Thinking processes
```

■ *Modules in CAP identified schools,* □ *Modules in randomly identified schools*
N = 62 modules. A number of interviewees attributed more than one thinking process to each module, thus the categories are not mutually exclusive.
Source: NFER interviews conducted with art teachers and heads of art departments (2003/2004).

Interviewees were questioned specifically about whether or not the module they were discussing demanded or provided any opportunities for analysis and evaluation. The National Curriculum key stage 3 objectives and GCSE requirements both cite analysing and evaluating art work as a priority and it was regarded as an important thinking process by the interviewees.

> *The curriculum allows them to have their own opinion, when looking at works of art and evaluating their own work. Their opinion is always valued, which is good for their self-esteem.*

Art teacher, randomly identified school

This GCSE requirement, and the interview question relating specifically to analysis and evaluation, may account for its ranking as the most common thinking process in the modules.

References to analysing and evaluating in modules in randomly identified schools included:

- analysing and evaluating artists work featured in 12 (35 per cent) of the modules
- analysing and evaluating their classmates and peers work featured in 20 (59 per cent) of the modules

- analysing and evaluating their own work featured in 32 (94 per cent) of the modules.

Further analysis of the data associated with the modules in randomly identified schools revealed the following information.

- Creating and making was the second most frequently mentioned category of thinking processes, mentioned in 22 (65 per cent) of the modules in the randomly identified schools.

- Processes associated with investigation and research were mentioned in relation to nine (26 per cent) of the modules in the randomly identified schools. As discussed in section 2.3.4, it is possible that research is fundamental to the work that is being done in the art curriculum, and that interviewees did not identify it as a distinct thinking process.

- Creative thinking processes featured least, mentioned in just 5 (15 per cent) of the modules in the randomly identified schools. This is perhaps again indicative of a skills-led approach to the curriculum, which focuses on the development of art form skills as opposed to broader creative thinking processes.

The figures given in Figure 2.5 show the range of thinking processes employed by pupils in both key stage 3 and 4 in the randomly selected schools. When the data was considered by key stage there was no significant differentiation.

Differences between modules in CAP and randomly identified schools

When the thinking processes identified in the modules in the randomly identified schools are compared with those identified in the modules in the CAP identified schools, the following observations can be made.

- All the interviewees in the CAP identified schools specified at least one thinking process for the module that their interview focused on, compared to 72 per cent of teachers in the randomly identified schools.

- In both cohorts of schools analysing and evaluating, and creating and making were the two most commonly cited categories.

- Investigating and researching was the least frequently mentioned category in the modules in the CAP identified schools, whereas creative thinking processes was the least referred to category in the randomly identified schools.

- Almost half of the modules in CAP identified schools (46 per cent) were identified as including creative thinking processes. This is significantly higher than for the modules in the randomly identified schools, where only 15 per cent were seen as featuring this group of thinking processes. Teachers in CAP identified schools were more likely to claim to encourage the development of creative thinking processes by providing flexible briefs for projects, avoiding the dictation of ideas and encouraging pupils to work beyond school art clichés.

We do tell them 'that's been done so many times before' or 'that's a bit predictable or obvious, lets move beyond it' – so it's a lot about pushing and challenging boundaries.
Art teacher, CAP identified school

2.4 Other curriculum features

In addition to the four elements of curriculum content discussed in section 2.3, interviewees were also asked to comment on the following areas:

- the use of external resources to support the curriculum
- any issues raised in the curriculum (for example, political, environmental or social)
- any links made with other curriculum areas.

2.4.1 The use of external resources to support the curriculum

Three main external resources were used to support the curriculum in the sample schools: internet, galleries and visiting artists. Each of these is explored in turn, with an overview of other emerging external resources at the end of this section.

Internet

The internet was the most common external resource cited, used to support the curriculum by both teachers and pupils in 16 (47 per cent) of the modules in the randomly identified schools and 18 (64 per cent) of the modules in the CAP identified schools. Interviewees commented that the internet presented opportunities for allowing pupils easy and instant access to a range of artists and artistic references.

The internet has opened up a whole new world – there are so many different artist websites now.
Art teacher, CAP identified school

Despite its popularity as a research tool, a significant proportion of interviewees expressed their reservations about its widespread use. There was an emerging concern that instead of increasing research skills, it actually deskilled pupils. There was a perception that pupils had a tendency to print out chunks of text relating to artists direct from websites, without conducting any critical analysis of their work for themselves.

> *I don't mind them using the internet for images, but I don't like them getting information on artists because they print it out and don't read it – it's a waste of time. They learn how to access information, but it doesn't serve any purpose. I want them to find out why the images are the way they are, not when the artist was born, married and how may children he had.*
> Head of department, randomly identified school

Research was not identified as a specific skill taught in art lessons by the majority of interviewees (see section 2.3.4) and internet research was referred to as something frequently undertaken by pupils in their own time. Thus, it is possible that the opportunity to develop pupils' ability to use the internet as a constructive research tool was being missed. One interviewee suggested the need for a website that would allow pupils access to a wide range of artists and art works, whilst encouraging them to investigate further and question the information presented.

Galleries

Only three modules (9 per cent) in randomly identified schools included visits to galleries, all of which were key stage 4 modules. Five modules (18 per cent) in the CAP identified schools included visits to galleries, again all of these were in key stage 4.

> *It's not that we don't want to take the key stage 3 students. It's just that if we do get any funding for visits, we tend to take the GCSE students instead.*
> Head of department, randomly identified school

The exhibitions visited were not always directly related to the work being done in the module, but were seen as a useful addition to the whole package of art education being taught.

Teachers from both cohorts stressed that they would often recommend galleries and appropriate exhibitions that the pupils may wish to visit independently. The extent to which these recommendations were followed

- television programmes recorded and used for art history (for example *on Art* series featuring Rolf Harris).

2.4.2 Issue-based work in the art curriculum

In their discussion of a particular module or project, interviewees were asked the module referred to any issues (political, social and environmental), or if the pupils raised any issues themselves. There was a general consensus that certain modules lent themselves more readily to the exploration of issues as opposed to those modules that were primarily based on skills and techniques. For example modules on 'self' and 'identity' frequently provided opportunities for the discussion of personal issues such as identity, families, relationships and social background, whereas modules focusing on the use of materials such as 'clay' included little or no reference to the exploration of issues. The exploration of issues featured more prevalently in key stage 4.

> *In general I don't feel year 7 are mature enough to handle certain issues. We start doing that at year 9 and onwards and from year 10 onwards we would expect that as part of the criteria.*
> Art teacher, CAP identified school

The issues raised in the curriculum, as delivered in the sample schools, were wide ranging and included AIDS, death, families, relationships, environmental issues, multicultural issues, charitable causes, phobias, memories, drugs, abortion, domestic violence and feminism.

The exploration of issues featured in various ways.

- **Issues were raised through the context of a piece of art work** – for example, a number of teachers used Picasso's Guernica as an artistic reference and discussed its portrayal of the miseries of war (cited in modules from five randomly identified and two CAP identified schools).

- **Issues were raised by looking at particular artists and genres** – for example, one module used the work of Keith Haring which led to a discussion of AIDS and the 1980s culture in which he produced his work. pop art often led to discussions of consumerism and mass culture (cited in modules from two randomly identified and three CAP identified schools).

- **Issues were raised through the study of art from a range of cultures** – for example, the beliefs system evident in Aboriginal art and the religious

depended on the individual pupils, parental influences and the pr[oximity of]
the school to a suitable gallery.

Visiting artists

No modules in the randomly identified schools included the use of
visiting artists. Two modules in the CAP identified schools had involv[ed]
artists, both sourced from local galleries. In one module the artist w[orked with]
the pupils for the duration of a module, accompanying them to colle[ct at]
the local beach and developing this into pieces of art over a series of [sessions. In]
the other module the pupils took part in a workshop at the local gal[lery which]
supported an exhibition they had gone to see.

In addition to these examples, teachers in the CAP identified schools [were more]
likely to refer to the use of external artists in other modules or in the [future]
than their colleagues in the randomly identified schools. One CA[P identified]
school had its own gallery on the school premises and the artists disp[laying]
work in this space often ran workshops for the pupils. A second sch[ool worked]
closely with two partnership artists from the city art gallery who ca[me into the]
school every week to work with different classes.

The majority of interviewees felt that both gallery visits and the use [of external]
artists were important additions to the curriculum and something the[y wished]
to access more frequently, but were restricted by timetabling, fundi[ng and]
logistical issues. Possible reasons for the discrepancies in the use [of external]
resources between the CAP identified and the randomly identified [schools are]
also explored in Chapter 3.

Other external resources

Other external resources used in both the randomly and CAP ident[ified schools]
included:

- artefacts collected by the teachers and brought into schools a[s a basis for]
  observational drawing
- photographs of the local area and other landscapes
- postcards collected from various museums and galleries
- videos used as stimuli for work (for example, a video documenti[ng]
  world events used as a stimulus for a project entitled Life Events[)]

significance of Islamic patterns (cited in modules from two randomly identified and four CAP identified schools).

- **Issues were raised by the students themselves** – for example, in relation to work they were doing, or work they had found by other artists (cited in modules from four randomly identified and five CAP identified schools).

- **Issues were used as a stimulus for art work** – for example, pupils in one module were asked to produce a piece of work based on personal fear and phobias. Another project required the pupils to research a charity for which they could design a piece of art work (cited in modules from four randomly identified and five CAP identified schools).

A number of modules featured the exploration of issues in more than one way, thus, the categories are not mutually exclusive.

In conclusion, the exploration of issues through the teaching of art appears to be more widespread in the CAP identified schools (featuring in 57 per cent of modules in CAP identified schools compared to 34 per cent of modules in the randomly identified schools). This may be interpreted as a further indication of a broad based curriculum, focusing on teaching through art as well as developing art skills, which has emerged as more prevalent within this cohort. However, the difference in the actual number of citation between the two cohorts was relatively low suggesting that limited weight should be attached to this finding.

2.4.3 Links with other parts of the school curriculum

The final element explored in this chapter is the extent to which teachers felt that the art curriculum that they taught linked to other curriculum areas. This section focuses on the cross-curricular links made by teachers, both intentionally and coincidentally, and any links made by the students themselves. Twenty-four per cent of interviewees (7 teachers in randomly identified schools and 6 in CAP identified schools), felt that the curriculum they delivered in art linked to the content of the curriculum in other subject areas.

Conscious and purposeful links, through cross-departmental planning, were evident in the following areas:

- citizenship and personal, social and health education (PSHE) (in three modules)

- English (in two modules). The development of literacy skills were frequently identified as an outcome of the art curriculum delivered, presumably because links to literacy as a key skill are a requirement of lesson plans

- Religious Education (in two modules)
- other arts subjects (in two modules).

Unintentional and unplanned links were identified in history, through art history and consideration of historical periods (in two modules); and geography, through map and diagram drawing and landscape or environment-based projects (in one module). In these cases teachers discovered the art module they were teaching linked with work being done in other subject areas through discussions with students or with colleagues once the schemes of work were underway. Thus, any cross-referencing was not planned or formally written into the scheme of work.

It was recognised by the majority of teachers that cross-departmental planning was not always possible, and that inhibitors such as the National Curriculum and restrictive GCSE syllabuses, claimed by interviewees as more of a restriction in other subject areas than in art, limited the amount of cross-curricular links to the art curriculum.

> *I think cross-curricular activities are important and that we should have more time to pursue them. But I think there isn't enough slack in the system now and people are worried about SAT* [Standard Assessment Test] *results and so they stick to their own subjects.*
> Art teacher, randomly identified school

Very little evidence emerged of planned links with other curriculum areas but interviewees were able to identify actual or potential links, which emerged on reflection in the interviews, suggesting there is a greater opportunity for cross-curricular working within the art curriculum than is currently being exploited.

Summary

Analysis of the data collected in the randomly identified schools gives an indication of the prevalent art curriculum in secondary schools. Distinct characteristics have emerged relating to the media and materials used in the curriculum, the references and resources used to support the curriculum and the underlying design principles that inform the curriculum.

The next section considers the nature and status of contemporary art practice within this curriculum.

2.5 The nature and status of contemporary art practice within school art

2.5.1 The nature of contemporary art practice within school art

Although one focus of this study was the place of contemporary art practice in school art, a choice was made not to work with a predetermined definition of contemporary art, in order to avoid closing down responses. The sponsors and their nominees identified schools that they thought engaged in contemporary art practice without reference to a shared definition. Researchers subsequently have established a grounded definition of characteristics that became apparent in those schools (based on the analysis of the modules discussed earlier). While some of these characteristics may have been apparent to varying degrees in some of the modules in randomly identified schools, they were significantly more prevalent in the CAP identified schools. Although some schools expressed commitment to a philosophical approach associated with contemporary art practice (see Chapter 4), this chapter explores only their practice.

A list of characteristics is now presented, and examples are used to illustrate the ways in which these characteristics featured within the sample of CAP identified schools.

Pupils produced work using ICT and other, less traditional media

Evidence of the use of ICT emerged only in modules in CAP identified schools. The use of other, less traditional media was also more prevalent in this cohort.

> A year 11 module from a CAP identified school provides an example of the use of ICT in the art curriculum. The module in question focused on the work of Eva Hesse and Max Ernst and the metamorphosis of natural and mechanical forms. Pupils' initial observational drawings both of natural and mechanical objects were scanned into the computer. Through the use of Photoshop the pupils were able to digitally manipulate their sketches to create metamorphosed images. These images were then used as pieces of art work in themselves and as stimuli for further work in various media including collage, frottage and clay.

> The use of other less traditional media was again evident in a key stage 4 module (this time a year 10 module). The aim of this module was the exploration of surface and texture. The pupils began by making observational sketches of natural materials, such as wood and stone, and considered the marks, patterns and shapes that make up their surface texture. Working on new and unusual materials including cloth, chipboard and chamois leather, pupils were encouraged to recreate the patterns of the natural surfaces using a range of painting techniques (for example, pouring, flicking and stippling). Although paint can be seen as a traditional or common art material, by applying it to surfaces other than paper and canvas pupils had the opportunity to work in more unusual media. This project also included the use of Photoshop for digital manipulation of the initial observational drawings.

Teachers used artistic references from the latter 20th and early 21st centuries to support the curriculum

The use of artistic references from the latter 20th and early 21st centuries was cited by over half of the interviewees in the CAP identified schools and was often used in conjunction with references from other historical periods to provide a wide overview of artistic movements. The use of such artistic references was frequently associated with the exploration of issues.

> A module on graffiti art used the work of Keith Haring and Jean-Michel Basquiat, both leading artists in the 1980s graffiti scene. The work of both artists focused on the culture in which they were living. Basquiat's work explored the 1980s drug culture and Haring produced a body of work for AIDS charities – both were prominent issues of the time. Tragically, both artists died in 1988 in their early thirties, as a direct result of the subject that they painted; Basquiat from a heroin overdose and Haring from the AIDS virus.
>
> By using artists whose work is so evidently issue based, the pupils were provided with an opportunity to think about and discuss the context and meaning of the images they were shown.
>
> *When issues like that come out through an art project, through something that they are engaged with, they don't seem to have a problem with – they are keen to discuss it and they seemed to understand that's why the works looked the way they did.*
> Head of department, CAP identified school

> By considering the issues in these works and the techniques used to convey meaning (such as the use of text and image combined) the pupils were able to think about their own culture and how they might represent this within their own work as well as developing their skills in the form of graffiti-style application of paint (including concepts of accident and incident).
>
> While Basquiat and Haring were the main references used, the pupils also looked at the art of ancient cultures including Egyptian, Aboriginal and African art. They looked specifically at the signs and symbols used to communicate meaning in these genres and how these can be compared to communication in contemporary art.

International artists and female artists were included in the artistic references used to support the curriculum

As discussed, the use of international art/culture appeared primarily to be the use of cultural imagery (for example, Islamic pattern), as opposed to individual artists of international origin.

> A year 8 module on Aboriginal art used the genre as a way of exploring art skills and techniques and the Aboriginal culture. The module was introduced to the pupils through an initial exploration of the concept of 'dreamtime', and the beliefs of the Aboriginal people. The pupils were then shown examples of Aboriginal art work, including some contemporary pieces, and explored the use of symbols, signs, colour and the representation of animals.
>
> As a stimulus for their own pieces, the pupils wrote short stories in which they imagined they were an Aborigine and documented the things that this Aborigine saw on a journey through the outback. The final pieces were based on a moment from these stories and incorporated the features of Aboriginal art they had seen in the examples.
>
> While the pupils were working on their paintings the teacher read out 'dreamtime' stories and played a CD of Aboriginal music. In this example, the pupils were provided with an opportunity to widen their understanding of art from another culture, but also to immerse themselves within the culture to develop their understanding of the context in which the art had been produced.

Whilst international art/culture was often used to teach cultural education as well as develop arts skills, there was no evidence in the data collected through teacher interviews of the use of women artists to explore women's studies and feminism.

> One pupil interviewed had produced a piece of work for GCSE coursework, which explored the theme of domestic violence, inspired by the work of Barbara Kruger. Through her initial research of the artist the pupil had not only developed her understanding of how Kruger combined image and text to portray meaning, a technique recreated in her final GCSE piece, but also her understanding of the issues addressed in Kruger's work.

Teachers included a wide range of art forms in the references used to support the curriculum

On average, interviewees in the CAP identified schools used twice as many art form references to support the curriculum as their colleagues in the randomly identified schools. In some schools the range far exceeded the average.

> One module looked at natural forms in art and how the natural world had inspired a range of artists. The skills and techniques being taught through this module were primarily fine art based, concentrating on colour mixing, the formal elements, observational drawing and the application of paint. However, the teacher delivering the module was keen to provide some context to the work by showing the importance of natural forms in art. This was done by exposing the pupils to a range of artists and art images that are based on, or inspired by natural forms. The range of art forms included architecture (Gaudi), fashion design (Issey Miyake), sculpture (Anish Kapoor and Andy Goldsworthy), painting (Georgia O'Keefe), jewellery design (Helen Smythe) and photography (Richard Long).
>
> By liaising with other members of staff in the department, the interviewee had been able to put together a comprehensive collection of artists and images that provided the pupils with a wide overview of the forms art can take.
>
> *We are forever adding to this collection of artists as people are continually inspired by natural forms. That way the pupils have a wider overview of art and the ways in which we can use natural forms.*
> Art teacher, CAP identified school
>
> In addition, the brief for this module had no set format for a final piece and allowed the pupils to experiment with a range of media and materials, and make a series of pieces in different form. This further increased the opportunities for the pupils to explore their understanding of what art can be.

Expression of meaning through art was taught as a distinct skill

Expressing meaning through art was taught as a skill in five modules in the CAP identified schools and included giving art work dramatic impact (creating mood through tone and colour), portraying a particular viewpoint on an issue and conveying a narrative.

> In one year 9 module the pupils looked at photographs (primarily photojournalism) and paintings of world events from history and the way in which the images represent not just the event itself but the artist's perspective on that event.
>
> *This is done through discussions with fellow pupils. They ask each other 'What are the feelings you are getting out of this?'.*
> Art teacher, CAP identified school
>
> The pupils are then asked to write down two events from their own lives, one good and one bad, and select one as a stimulus for a piece of art. The overall aim was for the pupils' feelings and emotions associated with their chosen event to be evident in their final pieces.

Teachers encouraged pupils to use and develop creative thinking processes

The creative thinking processes identified by interviewees in the CAP identified schools included giving personal responses to the module brief, experimenting both with materials and ideas and thinking conceptually. Modules featuring these thinking processes were characterised by teachers acting intentionally as facilitators and encouraging pupils to think 'outside the box', avoid clichés and allow for mistakes to become part of the work.

> One interviewee, in describing the processes involved in a year 9 module, highlighted the way in which the pupils were encouraged to think creatively in order to come up with ideas for a final piece, rather than predetermining what it is they want to produce.
>
> *It's trying to get them used to that process of 'How do you generate ideas just by changing and doing?'. They still have this idea that you can sit there and come up with a final piece – I'm trying to show them that surprising things can happen as you go along a journey – you can go off at tangents, and discover things you didn't think you would.*
> Head of department, CAP identified school

In a further example, pupils were encouraged to experiment with a range of 2D materials, including oil pastels, coloured pencils, crayons and paints, and to explore the properties of the materials as a way of developing a final piece. The interviewee discussing this module noted that it was a process the pupils were initially uncomfortable with but which ultimately allowed them the freedom to develop ideas through experimentation and allowing the materials themselves to dictate what the final image should look like.

> *Most would say: 'Miss, it's gone wrong!' And I'd say: 'But has it? Why don't you scratch into it?'. That would get them really involved – I think they come to school thinking that's the way you do it, and they need to learn not to be precious about the work and learn to have freedom.*
> Art teacher, CAP identified school

The curriculum taught included visits to galleries and museums and included the use of external artists

Visits to galleries and museums and the use of external artists appeared to be a minority activity in school art as a whole. However, a number of examples did emerge in the CAP identified schools.

In one module the school had worked with a local digital artist, recommended by the local arts centre, to facilitate a project based on the use of debris and found materials. The education officer from the local arts centre also came in to assist with the project. The school was situated by the coast and the initial session involved the artist taking a group of pupils down to the beach to collect man-made and natural objects to bring back into school. These objects were then used for observational drawing and to make collage and relief pictures. Digital photographs of the compositions were taken and the pupils explored ways of manipulating these images using a range of computer packages.

Because of the limited number of computers and the limited amount of space in the computer suite, not all the pupils in the year group had the opportunity to work with the artist. However, the teachers in the department used the ideas and similar techniques with those pupils who were not included from the sessions at a later date. Thus, the use of an external artist in this example provided the pupils with the opportunity to work with a professional artist and also allowed the teachers to gain new ideas, skills and techniques relating to the use of ICT from observing the artist and learning from his expertise.

One CAP identified school in the sample had its own on-site art gallery, which is used by local and nationally known artists to display their work. Pupils were free to view the work displayed in the gallery in their own time as well as through structured visits during art lessons. The artists displaying work in the space often ran additional workshops for the pupils, allowing the pupils the chance to see the artists work first hand and gain an understanding of the meaning behind it and the techniques employed in creating it.

This school also had close links with the local art gallery and art education centre, run by the LEA, through a member of staff's additional role as an advanced skills teacher. Through these connections they were able to bring artists in frequently to work with pupils, with the aim of providing this opportunity for each pupil at least once a year, and provide regular opportunities for gallery visits, though these were not always directly related to the work that was being done in school.

If they go to an exhibition we don't expect them to use it directly in their work – it's more about engaging with art and soaking it up.
Art teacher, CAP identified school

A further example of the use of galleries and museums was a module that included a visit to a gallery at the very start of the project. In contrast to the approach outlined above, in this case the exhibition then acted as a direct stimulus for the pupils work. In the module being discussed the exhibition was the work of the sculptor Eva Hesse, and the rest of the module was influenced by her work. In previous years the same module had been taught on the same theme (metamorphosis) but a different exhibition and artist had been used as the initial stimulus and the work produced in the module had been adapted accordingly.

What we do with this module is to look and see what exhibition is on and adapt it to fit with that.
Art teacher, CAP identified school

The characteristics discussed were more prevalent in the modules in the CAP identified schools, suggesting they were features of the art curriculum taught in this cohort. The nature of the characteristics reflects the broad and balanced approach to the curriculum prevalent in the underlying design principles in the CAP identified schools (see section 2.2.1), inclusive of a range of media, materials and artistic references, providing opportunities for gallery visits and incorporating new ideas.

Comparisons with existing research

The characteristics of contemporary art practice in schools identified above are based entirely on the data collected. Within the existing research and current thinking on art education there were few attempts to define contemporary art practice in schools. Emery (2002b) defined a framework for contemporary (defined as postmodernist) art practice, based on observations of practice in schools in Australia and the UK. Included in her suggested orientations for a contemporary art education framework was the idea that students are exposed to high and low art (fine art and popular art), multicultural art and art by lesser known artists. This resonates with the use of international and women artists and contemporary art references in the modules in the CAP identified schools in this research. Emery's framework also makes reference to the study of art for different purposes and art created in a variety of materials. The characteristics of contemporary art practice identified in this study include the use of ICT and other less traditional materials and references to architecture, fashion design jewellery design and other art forms in the CAP identified schools. Finally, Emery identifies the study of 'art for meaning'. This orientation was evident in a proportion of the modules in the CAP identified schools studied here, in that expression of meaning through art was sometimes taught as a distinct skill.

The findings of this research therefore reinforce the orientations identified by Emery. The similarities between the characteristics of CAP identified schools in this research and the orientations of contemporary art education identified by Emery suggest that contemporary art practice in schools, although perhaps not easily definable, is recognisable and distinguishable from more 'typical' practices.

The teachers' perspective on contemporary art practice

It was also the case that no definition of contemporary art practice was provided for the interviewees in the CAP identified schools. However, they were asked to describe the way in which contemporary art figured in their department's overall approach. Their responses are considered in this section in order to draw out any similarities or discrepancies between their responses and the characteristics discussed earlier.

A number of teachers cited more than one approach, thus the categories discussed are not mutually exclusive.

Just over a third of the teachers interviewed felt that the contemporary influence was primarily reflected in the range of artistic references that they used to support the curriculum. Often contemporary artists and art works were used alongside, or in comparison to more traditional references, rather than as an alternative. Indeed, the data indicates that significantly more modules in the CAP identified schools use artistic references from the latter 20th and early 21st century, including conceptual and installation art and any art produced from 1970 to the present day, which may be classified as contemporary.

Six interviewees commented that contemporary art practices featured more strongly in key stage 4 and above. When the differentiation between modules is considered in key stages 3 and 4, in the CAP identified schools, the range of art forms used to support the curriculum was higher at key stage 4. Print, photography and installation all feature more prevalently at key stage 4 than at key stage 3. They each feature in 20 per cent of key stage 4 modules, compared to approximately 10 per cent of key stage 3 modules. However, there was no further evidence that the contemporary art characteristics, discussed earlier, featured more prominently post key stage 3.

Five interviewees felt that bringing in external artists, or providing opportunities for visiting galleries, contributed to the inclusion of contemporary art practice in their departments. As discussed in section 2.4, the use of external resources of this nature did feature more in the CAP identified schools.

The use of a wide range of materials, including the use of more contemporary materials, was identified by a further four interviewees. Contemporary media were identified by these interviewees primarily as ICT and digital media. Analysis of the media and materials used in the curriculum in both cohorts of schools supports this, in that modules using ICT appeared only in the CAP identified schools.

Two interviewees, both from the same school, referred to the way in which the students were encouraged to experiment with materials and allow the materials' property to dictate the final product as a contemporary approach to making art.

2.5.2 The status of contemporary art practice within randomly identified schools

The characteristics set out in section 2.5.1 were identified as more prevalent in the CAP identified schools. This section explores each identified characteristic and the extent to which it featured in the modules described in the randomly identified schools included in the research. As the modules discussed by teachers in the ten randomly selected schools might be seen as indicative of a more 'typical' curriculum, this may give an indication of the status of contemporary art within schools in general.

Pupils produced work using ICT and other, less traditional media

The use of ICT did not feature in any modules in the randomly identified schools. Other, less traditional materials featured in just two modules in the randomly identified schools.

Teachers used artistic references from the latter 20th and early 21st century to support the curriculum

Artistic references from this time period were used in just four of the modules in the randomly identified schools.

International artists and women artists were included in the artistic references used to support the curriculum

No modules in the randomly identified schools used international artists or art genres as references to support the curriculum and only two modules included the work of women artists (Georgia O'Keefe and Bridget Reilly).

Teachers included a wide range of art forms in the references used to support the curriculum

The modules in the randomly identified schools used an average of just one art form in the references used to support the curriculum – this was predominately paintings.

Expression of meaning through art was taught as a distinct skill

Expression of meaning was only cited as a distinct skill that the pupils were learning in two of the modules in the randomly identified schools.

Teachers encouraged pupils to use and develop creative thinking processes

Creative thinking processes were explicitly identified in five modules in the randomly identified schools.

The curriculum included visits to galleries and museums and included the use of external artists

Just three modules in randomly identified schools included visits to galleries and there were no examples in this cohort of the pupils working with a professional artist.

This report does not wish to suggest that the characteristics associated with schools reputed to embrace contemporary art practice are entirely absent from art departments as a whole. Indeed, of the ten schools in the sample of randomly identified schools, two appeared to share more characteristics with the CAP identified schools than did the other randomly identified schools, indicating that the range of levels of inclusion of contemporary art practice varies between schools. However, the data suggests that contemporary art practice, as an element of school art, does not feature strongly in the curriculum for most schools, and that its presence in most schools may be marginal. At the other extreme, no school had embraced contemporary art practice to the total exclusion of the more 'typical' curriculum approaches.

2.6 Summary and conclusions

Based on the analysis of the data collected in the randomly identified schools, the art curriculum taught in schools can be seen to be characterised by:

- the prevalent use of painting and drawing as the medium in which pupils work
- the prevalent use of artistic references from the early 20th century
- the prevalent use of male, European artists, predominantly painters
- the importance placed on development of art form skills, including the use of art materials, the development of specific techniques and observational drawing skills
- the teaching of the formal elements of art
- the creation of opportunities for pupils to think in an analytical and evaluative way, whilst employing thinking processes associated with creating and making art
- the use of the internet, more than books and other resources, for researching artists and art history
- limited use of galleries, museums or professional artists and artists in residence
- limited opportunities for using art to explore issues (though more opportunities emerged at key stage 4)

- limited cross-curricular working and inter-departmental planning
- limited use of artistic references from before 1800 and from the latter 20th and early 21st century
- limited opportunities for pupils to produce art work using ICT
- limited requirement of pupils to engage in creative thinking processes.

A number of differences between the curricula as taught at key stages 3 and 4 emerged:

- evidence emerged of a more balanced use of 2D and 3D materials at key stage 4
- artists and works of art before 1800, or art between the wars were referred to in key stage 3 modules only
- early 20th century and abstract art in Europe featured more prevalently in key stage 4 modules
- research skills taught in a higher proportion of key stage 4 modules (presumably because of the emphasis placed on research within the assessment criteria for GCSE)
- the exploration of issues featured more prevalently in key stage 4
- all references to gallery visits were for pupils in key stage 4.

Analysis of the curriculum by key stage reflects the common underlying design principles adopted by the majority of schools, in which exploratory and experimental processes, frequently associated with more independent, learning chronologically follow the acquisition of art making skills.

The following characteristics were more likely to be reported in the CAP identified cohort of schools:

- pupils produced work using ICT and other, less traditional media
- teachers used artistic reference from the latter 20th and early 21st century to support the curriculum
- international artists and women artists were included in the artistic references used to support the curriculum
- teachers included a wide range of art forms in the references used to support the curriculum
- expression of meaning through art was taught as a distinct skill

- teachers encouraged pupils to use and develop creative thinking processes
- the curriculum included visits to galleries and museums and included the use of external artists.

The nature of these characteristics reflects a broader and more balanced approach to the curriculum prevalent in the underlying design principles in the CAP identified schools. However, it is worth noting that these characteristics may not be specifically about contemporary art practice. For example, the use of a wider range of artistic references and the use of a wide range of media and materials may be more indicative of a broad and balanced curriculum as a whole. The exploration of art as a visual communication tool may be more indicative of a curriculum that is less concerned with artistic technique and skill.

Strong evidence of contemporary art practice did not feature in many of the schools in the sample; furthermore, in schools where it did feature, in no case did it displace conventional art teaching approaches. Where it was introduced, it was often in conjunction with more conventional practices. The presumption in the majority of the schools was of a need to teach skills and techniques before the issues and concepts within art can be addressed.

Two distinct underlying design principles determining the content of the art curriculum emerged from interviewees' descriptions of their overall approach to the curriculum and of the content of individual art modules. The more prevalent approach to art teaching emerged as a directed approach in which the initial emphasis is on the development of art skills. This progressed to the introduction of more exploratory and experimental processes, frequently associated with more independent learning, at key stage 4. The second approach, more prevalent in the CAP identified schools, was characterised by a broader based curriculum, which was both pupil and teacher centred, building on the premise of skills but integrating more creative and conceptual thinking, exploratory work, the exploration of issues in art and awareness of art as a visual communication tool.

Questions for policy makers and practitioners

The following questions have been framed in response to the findings discussed in this chapter.

- Is there an over reliance on painting and drawing to the exclusion of other media – such as sculpture, design and photography – and what are the educational repercussions of this?

- Is the limited creative use of ICT in art, as opposed to its use for art research, a shortcoming given the emphasis placed on the use of ICT within the curriculum as a whole?
- Should efforts be made to achieve a greater integration of skills development and the exploration of meaning, issues and context? Does the teaching of skills exclude the exploration of meaning, issues and context?
- Should it be assumed that the exploration of meaning, issues and expression should chronologically follow the acquisition of art making skills?
- Is sufficient attention being paid in art to the teaching of research skills, and in particular the critical use of the internet?
- Would art education be more effective if it were to embrace a wider range of artistic references to support the curriculum, including references from the latter 20th and early 21st century?
- Are the characteristics or features found to be more prevalent in the CAP identified schools indicative of the inclusion of contemporary art practice or of a broad, balanced and inclusive approach to art teaching?

3 Factors influencing the choice of art curriculum content

3.1 Introduction

Chapter 2 revealed some significant findings concerning the content of the art curriculum taught in secondary schools, gleaned from teachers' descriptions of the modules as taught. The research also sought to ascertain the factors that might influence decisions concerning that content, specifically those made at school and teacher level. Interviews with heads of departments and art teachers included a number of approaches to address this issue.

- Interviewees were asked about their own professional background and training, since it was deemed that these might have some impact on curriculum choices.

- They were asked about the school and department context and to outline their understanding of the department's overall approach to the art curriculum.

- They were directly asked what they themselves thought were the key influences and inhibitors in making curriculum content choices.

- In the case of class teachers, and for heads of department where time permitted, interviewees were asked to respond to a small selection of art images and comment on their suitability for inclusion in the curriculum.

Rather than report responses to each of these different types of data gathering approaches, this chapter starts with:

- factors related to the wider context, that is, the nationally prescribed curriculum (section 3.2), and gradually focuses down through

- the school context (section 3.3)

- the department context (section 3.4)

- resource availability (section 3.5)

- factors related to the teacher as an individual (section 3.6).

There follows a report on the somewhat more experimental approach of eliciting the responses of teachers to particular images of art (section 3.7).

The chapter concludes with a summary of the findings relating to factors affecting curriculum choice (section 3.8).

3.2 Perceptions of the enabling or inhibiting effects of the nationally prescribed art curriculum

Since 1988 the art curriculum in secondary schools has been taught in the context of the National Curriculum. In the earliest days, while the art teaching community was encouraged that art had been included as a subject, this response had been moderated by a fear that a level of prescription might inhibit teachers' ability to define what was taught and in what way. The initial reaction of fear of prescription was ameliorated after the Dearing Report (1994), at which point the prescribed 'canon' of artistic examples for each of the art forms was dropped, and the present position of defining attainment targets, rather than delivery methods, became the preferred approach.

When asked whether the National Curriculum was a limitation on the choice of curriculum content, the majority response (75 per cent) was no. Indeed, some interviewees commended the enabling quality of existing curriculum requirements. The prevailing view was that the curriculum was appropriately open to interpretation by individual teachers or departments.

> *You've got your set guidelines, but it's not strict.*
> Art teacher, randomly identified school

> *It's very general – you can apply it to almost anything.*
> Art teacher, randomly identified school

There were, however, dissenting voices, expressing the view that the curriculum was restrictive in itself. One interviewee challenged the requirement that all pupils' work have artist references and provide evidence of working process, precluding the possibility of a talented pupil 'starting from the other end' (though some comments suggested that many do). Another teacher, asked what factors limited the choice of curriculum content, replied as follows.

> *I think probably just the whole National Curriculum. We don't just sort of do fun things whenever we want to. It needs to sort of have a purpose and lead somewhere. It is restrictive.*
> Art teacher, randomly identified school

While no other teacher took such an explicitly libertarian view, the importance of the enjoyment element of art as a choice factor, should not be overlooked and is alluded to in other parts of this report (see section 3.2.2).

Three other teachers referred to restrictions on gifted pupils, who might be working in a much more original way, or wishing to work in media that could not be accommodated by the curriculum.

Only 11 per cent of interviewees were of the view that the assessment requirements, either those in place within the school or as part of the GCSE system, were an inhibiting factor. Some referred to sophisticated systems for assessment, others to the natural and habitual process of assessment in school art.

> *We have the* [named] *computer assessment, linked to the assessment office. Twice a year we give individual assessment for organisation, effort, behaviour, homework and progress.*
> Art teacher, randomly identified school

> *Assessment is not a problem – they do that naturally anyway. Teaching art, you are walking around seeing what they are doing all the time. We have two week assessment modules at the end of every term.*
> Art teacher, randomly identified school

Again there were dissenting voices.

> *Because we are getting all the students to meet all the assessment criteria,* [it] *means that sometimes we can't try out all the ideas we might want to develop.*
> Art teacher, randomly identified school

Another teacher had ambivalent thoughts about the conformity demanded by the assessment process.

> *Assessment is hard to do, but not restrictive as to what we do. I suppose it is in a way, in that they all have to have a similar outcome so that we can assess the clay box or the watch we are going to make this year. They can't all go off at a tangent, which would be lovely. They need to know and show the skills, but I don't think that restricts in any way.*
> Art teacher, CAP identified school

It is notable that this teacher referred to the presentation of skills for assessment, rather than, for example, the freedom to explore ideas, and that she/he did not regard this as a restriction. Although very few interviewees felt that assessment might restrict or inhibit curriculum choices, it is possible that the assessment procedure is so fundamentally grounded in the examination and qualification process that most teachers are no longer aware of the restrictions resulting from an assessment process. Only when a dissenting view is expressed does the possibility emerge that many teachers may be blind to an inhibition that may be affecting them all.

> *Assessment is full of jargon and time consuming and I would like to see it changed. It totally affects what you're teaching – you have to plan your whole project around those assessment objectives or they are not going to get the GCSE.*
> Art teacher, CAP identified school

Assessment is an inevitable component of any process culminating in an examination or qualification. It is, arguably, inevitable that it should affect the process and content of teaching. However, the fact that most teachers do not perceive it to be restrictive may indicate that they agree with the prescribed criteria and processes of assessment. The statment that 'they all have to have similar outcomes' or that 'they can't all go off at a tangent' is perhaps seen by many as an inevitable and unquestionable aspect of an art curriculum. Does a skill-centred curriculum inevitably lead to similar outcomes or preclude tangential trajectories? This view is not universally shared, raising the question: Is this a self-imposed restriction, or an almost (but not completely) irresistible outcome of following a curriculum?

3.3 The school context

The ethos of the school was not seen by any interviewees to in any way inhibit their choice of curriculum content. Although one teacher referred to the fact that she avoided references to drugs and alcohol, it was not clear whether this was a school edict or a personal decision – no other member of that staff expressing a similar constraint. One interviewee expressed the view that far from being inhibited by the school ethos, the art department was far more likely to be a positive influence on the school ethos.

However, seven teachers (13 per cent) did choose to refer to the nature of the pupils and their background as an inhibitor. Lack of 'cultural understanding' or exposure to art, lack of understanding and support from parents, and poor behaviour, especially amongst boys, were all seen as inhibitors, though it is unclear how this last factor affected curriculum choice rather than curriculum delivery. Two referred to lack of ability in art, though one of these went on to point out that this, after all, was why the pupils were at school and studying art! The issue of pupil (and in some cases parent) responses to particular art works did not emerge during this part of the interviews, but will be referred to when discussing teacher reactions to a selection of images (see section 3.2.2 below).

3.4 The art department context

It became apparent from interviews that the department ethos and modus operandi might be a significant factor in determining the choice of curriculum content by teachers. Chapter 2 reveals certain distinguishing features in the curriculum content of art departments perceived to incorporate contemporary art practices in their teaching.

As set out in Chapter 2, the orthodoxy of skills teaching in the early secondary years apparently pervades all schools, and therefore reflects a national assumption that this is the appropriate progression for learners. The most common departmental approach, having the greatest impact on curriculum content, was that of focusing on the acquisition and development of skills during key stage 3, leading to more exploratory work and greater 'independent learning', in key stage 4. But to what extent did such departmental approaches affect curriculum content choices by individual teachers?

Differences between CAP identified and randomly identified art departments

The attachment to skills teaching was forcefully expressed by many interviewees and was equally strongly supported both in CAP identified and randomly identified schools.

> *I think very much that in key stage 3 the pupils should have a good grounding in the fundamentals of art and I have a real belief in teaching skills because I think a lot of that got squeezed out.*
> Art teacher, randomly identified school

> *We value very highly the use of observational drawing as a starting point...*

you have to build in skills and techniques, but in an interesting way.
Head of department, CAP identified school

The frequency and forcefulness with which skill learning was referred to did not vary between the two cohorts of schools. Though not cited quite as frequently, the 'opportunity to work in a wide range of materials' was also cited, more frequently in CAP identified schools.

Contemporary art making is not always content driven – it is so often about the exploratory nature of finding out about material.
Head of department, CAP identified school

The greater tendency of heads of departments in CAP identified schools to refer to the nature of the pupil experience, and to the importance of ideas, current events and external stimuli, is reflected to some extent in the curriculum content chosen by teachers in those schools.

Year 9 splits into three projects [including] *personal spaces and public places. This year the topic coincided with the Saddam statue being torn down, so they designed a replacement, looking at symbolism – hope, peace, freedom – very spiritual and informally linked with PSHE.*
Head of department, CAP identified school

I think it's quite difficult giving them a traditional, thorough base in education, which is basically what we do in key stage 3, and key stage 4 is more a transition time. Key stage 5 is when we get them thinking about contemporary issues. I think it would be interesting to bring it down into key stage 3 and I think I've got some work to do on that.
Head of department, CAP identified school

The modules described in CAP identified schools reveal characteristics that corroborate those views, but not exclusively. Those schools also pay very considerable attention to the acquisition of art form skills. Not all teachers in CAP identified schools appeared to devise modules or content with these more CAP-oriented approaches in mind, while some teachers in randomly identified schools did. It would appear that a departmental approach might be influential, but not necessarily the exclusive influence. Indeed, in one CAP identified school, the very CAP-oriented approach of the head of department was not reflected in the discourse of other department staff. On the other hand, eight teachers referred to the importance of the collective knowledge of the department staff and their tendency to discuss and share views and knowledge about their teaching.

The conformity of teachers to departmental approaches

Both heads of departments and art teachers agreed that whatever the departmental approach, individual teachers were accorded a considerable amount of autonomy in defining the actual content of any module taught, in order to play to their own strengths and interests and to those of the pupils in their classes.

> *There is not a single class in school that does the same project as another or a project that has been done before... If you repeat a pattern year after year, which is exercise driven, then that stifles any potential creativity and diversity... It puts the teachers in a situation where they have to be creative.*
> Head of department, CAP identified school.

> *A lot of the things I do are generated from my own research rather than all being prescribed by exactly what the head of department lays down for me to do.*
> Art teacher, randomly selected school

Interviewees in only three schools spoke of the school's art curriculum plan (rather than national requirements) as restrictive for teachers. In a randomly selected school, the head of department explained that this was necessary because two members of staff were not specialist art teachers. In two CAP identified schools there was consensus between the heads of departments and the teachers that the curriculum established by the department was adhered to quite comprehensively, though in one of these, the head of department was keen to express a willingness for staff to 'have inputs in addition to this – we discuss it and see the impact'. The other head of department described the range of skills and materials to be covered in key stage 3, 'regardless of which teacher'. Both of these heads of department also described their key stage 3 modules as 'traditional'. This may not necessarily suggest that their modules were in fact more traditional than those in other schools, rather that the head of department was able to make such an observation, possibly comparing them with what they would ideally provide.

Collective departmental awareness of developments in CAP

Asked if they thought that the curriculum in their art department reflected developments in the art world, only 14 were of the definite view that it did. While only one claimed (or admitted) that it didn't, others were equivocal, believing that they went some way towards it, but could not be expected to keep fully up to date. Two interviewees felt that they could not expect, or be expected as school teachers to be 'at the cutting edge' of art knowledge. For others, the position was identified as 'Yes, but not enough' or 'Yes, but could do more' or even, 'Yes and no – better than in the past'. Teachers in randomly identified schools were more likely to be quite definite that they did keep up to date, with those in CAP identified schools being more circumspect. Unfortunately, the perceptual data from interviews could not be challenged or corroborated by other means.

Others presented reasons why they were not abreast of developments, or why their curriculum did not reflect developments in the art world, without admitting that they were not keeping up. 'Perhaps we're stuck in our ways – playing safe' or 'you teach what you are taught'. This type of response was epitomised by the following comments.

> *Yes, I think that we could perhaps, and that's down to again us perhaps more as individuals. We could do more to do with contemporary art and the issues that are dealt with there. I would say that perhaps some of that is to do with an age thing, the fact that there are three of us of a very similar age. We did have a colleague who has moved on now, who I actually valued because she was very much into what was happening in art now and her understanding of it and we used to have long conversations about it and that was always good. She was always bringing in new works of people I had never heard of and that kept me on top of it. Personally I feel I could be more on top of the art of today.*
> Art teacher, randomly identified school

Again, the significance of individual art teachers, and their role in mutual information updating, comes to the fore. Other interviewees described how their own familiarity with the art world enables pupil learning.

> *We talk about them with the children – things that children should know about what's going on in their society and how people react to what's going on. Looking at young British artists leads to discussions about what is art… School art is about both skills and concepts – you follow the interest of the individual children and try to keep a balance.*
> Art teacher, randomly identified school

> *Yes, I think we are more and more. We certainly use techniques, we certainly use ideas and we certainly challenge kids with new concepts. Less and less do I hear kids saying, when I take them to Tate Modern for example, 'What's this? This isn't art!' They aren't derogatory when they go there as much as they use to because it's cool to go to Tate Modern. So if you're there it must be cool then to try and interact with the works, engage with the works which they try and do more and more.*

Art teacher, randomly identified school

However, the desirability of keeping up with current art trends was not endorsed by all interviewees. Responses fell into two camps: those who dismissed the relevance of contemporary art to young people, and those for whom other aspects of art teaching took priority. One of the more experienced teachers explained that she/he hadn't the faintest idea what post-modern art was about, and doubted that anyone else did either, while another corroborated that view by admitting that she/he didn't understand contemporary art.

> *I suppose what we are limited in is our knowledge of the more obscure or conceptual artists. I wouldn't recommend Damien Hirst or other conceptual artists for pupils to work from as I'm not really sure what they would do with it.*

Head of department, randomly identified school

Others expressed the view that contemporary art was 'too conceptual and highbrow' or that 'kids don't respond to conceptual art'. There were further views that contemporary art was something that needed to wait its turn in the curriculum.

> *School is about teaching skills, and from there pupils go on to produce more conceptual work.*

Art teacher, randomly identified school

Lastly, one teacher explained that their department curriculum did not reflect current art development: 'It reflects what Office for Standards in Education (Ofsted) wants.'

How individual teachers and departments keep up with developments in the art world will be further discussed in section 3.6.2.

3.5 Resource influences

One might be surprised if, when asked what inhibited their curriculum content choices, teachers did not refer to inadequate resources. This section reveals those aspects of resourcing that most exercised their minds. Interviewee responses were analysed under the following headings, identified as emerging from their own discourse:

- space
- art materials
- art images
- computers
- access to galleries and artist studios
- time.

Space was by far the most cited material resource that inhibited curriculum content. Almost half of all interviewees cited this as an inhibition, often in conjunction with class sizes. Inadequate space was seen to affect the choice of activities and media used, either because of lack of space needed for the activity itself, or because of inadequate storage space for artefacts produced. It clearly restricted the scope for 3D work, but also for working in larger 2D formats. One school was suffering from not having specialist art teaching rooms. Interviewees from CAP and randomly identified schools were almost equally likely to cite space as an inhibiting factor.

Art materials, or the lack of funding to purchase them, were seen as an inhibitor by 16 (30 per cent) interviewees. There were references to the use of found objects as a means of counteracting this problem. Interviewees referred mainly to shortages of art materials. While funding shortages exercised the minds of some interviewees, an equal number of teachers made it clear that materials were not in short supply and shortage did not affect curriculum decisions adversely at all. Notably, interviewees from randomly identified schools were more than twice as likely as colleagues from CAP identified schools to report resource shortages as an inhibitor.

This might indicate that CAP identified schools are better resourced than randomly identified schools, or that teachers in those schools are less inhibited by resource implications. The data available does not enable researchers to identify any causal relationship. Does a good budget enable the incorporation of CAP, does the presence of CAP encourage better resourcing, or do both result from a higher status for art in the whole school curriculum?

Art images were generally seen to be sufficiently available, but with certain reservations. While almost any image could be found on the internet, reproducing them in sufficient quantity was sometimes prohibitively expensive, rendering their use impossible. School libraries were occasionally cited as sources of art images, with teachers referring to their limited capacity to cover the full range of art movements.

Computers for research purposes were in short supply in some schools, while readily available in others. There were also concerns about the regurgitation aspect of internet use, with pupils learning that they could simply reproduce images and text concerning an artist or art work without gaining any understanding. There was surprisingly little mention of the shortage of computers as a tool for making art, suggesting that there was very little appetite, at least amongst teachers, for computer aided art work in this sample of schools. (Computer aided art featured very rarely in the description of modules. If teachers did not refer to a shortage of computers as the reason for this, one might assume that the absence was the result of shortage of desire to engage with such work.)

Galleries and artist studios were seen as key resources by many teachers, and the shortage of funding to access them, along with the onerous procedures for obtaining health and safety clearance for visits out of school, were cited as restrictions in terms of curriculum content by three interviewees. Another referred to the fact that pupils 'would die rather than go to a gallery'. In contrast, five interviewees stated that resources were not an impediment to attending galleries and artists' studios.

Time, as for all subjects, was seen to restrict possibilities, and directly affected decisions concerning content in certain important ways. Where lessons were particularly short, the logistics of taking out and clearing away certain materials made teaching in those media virtually impossible. This could also have the effect of making projects 'drag on', with pupils losing sight of what they set out to achieve. One teacher referred to the vast amount of time lost to art teachers having to invigilate exams, especially since the introduction of AS level exams. In that particular school a total of 65 hours of teaching time for other year groups was lost, with specialist art teachers having to invigilate where in many other subjects non-specialists would suffice.

One interviewee referred to the reluctance of teachers in other subjects to release pupils for gallery visits. Again, randomly identified schools were almost twice as likely as CAP identified schools to cite time as an inhibiting factor. Whether this reflects the actual amount of time allocated to art in each cohort, or the attitudes of the interviewees to the management of time, is not apparent from the data.

3.6 Factors associated with individual teachers

Once the extent of the opportunity for teachers to adapt modules and schemes of work to suit their own skills and interests, supported by a willingness from heads of department that they do so had been established, the factors influencing individual teachers' curriculum choices become more significant.

This section begins with a summary of the training and experience of art teachers, and explores ways in which this may affect their curriculum content choices (section 3.6.1) This is followed by discussion of their responses to the question, 'What influences your choice of art genres, artists or images used in the curriculum?' (section 3.6.2).

3.6.1 The training and experience of art teachers and its possible impact on curriculum content choices

The academic background of the 36 class teachers and 18 heads of departments is summarised below. Table 3.1 also includes the percentages of interviewees who had previously worked as artists.

Teachers in CAP identified schools were somewhat more likely to have a fine art degree. Of the 23 teachers in all of the schools in the sample, 10 degrees were in fashion or textiles, six in graphic and other design subjects, and three in ceramics and the remainer had degress in fine art. These other qualifications were more prevalent in randomly identified schools. Heads of department were more likely to have a degree in fine art than were class teachers. References were made in interviews to the need for teachers to share their knowledge of artists, genres and examples, and the only individuals specifically identified by other teachers as sources of such information were those with fine art degrees.

Staff in CAP identified schools were more likely to have worked as professional artists before entering teaching. They tended to cite this as one of the factors enabling them to draw on a range of current artistic references, either because of their previous experience, or because it gave them greater access to other practising artists. (Chapter 2 indicated that departments in CAP identified schools were also more likely to introduce practising artists to their pupils.) Whether there is any inherent advantage in teachers having experience as a professional artist is not revealed by this research. It may well be that they are better able to inform pupils about the experience of art production if they have undertaken it over a period of time. The Artist Teacher Scheme, administered by the National Society for Education in Art and Design (NSEAD) and financially supported by ACE seeks to enable practising teachers to experience art production as well as to increase their knowledge and understanding of contemporary art and to 're-engage with their own thinking and personal development as artists' (Artist teacher scheme information). Thus, personal practice is regarded by NSEAD and ACE as a significant enhancement to the effectiveness of art teaching in schools.

Table 3.1 Graduate qualifications of art teachers and heads of department

Qualification/ experience	Percentage of teachers in CAP identified schools (number)	Percentage of teachers in randomly identified schools (number)	Percentage of heads of department in CAP identified schools (number)	Percentage of heads of department in randomly identified schools (number)
Fine art degree	44 (9)	36 (5)	50 (3)	60 (7)
Craft/textile/design degree	56 (12)	64 (10)	50 (3)	40 (5)
Worked or working as artist	39 (8)	17 (3)	25 (2)	5 (1)

N = 54: 21 teachers and 6 heads of department from CAP identified schools; 15 teachers and 12 heads of department and from randomly identified schools.
Teachers could cite more than one experience, so percentages may not sum to 100.
Source: NFER interviews conducted with art teachers and heads of art departments (2003/2004)

CPD as a means of updating art knowledge and skills was explored in the interviews. Courses related to GCSE examinations, especially concerning assessment and moderation, comprised the majority of CPD opportunities both for teachers and heads of department. These were seen as valuable as a means of finding out what other school art departments were doing. ICT courses, some of which referred specifically to art skills, were the next most undertaken CPD. Courses run by galleries were referred to particularly by heads of department rather than by art teachers, the reason for this is unclear. Six teachers referred to the importance of mutual support within the department as a means of professional development, but there was a marked absence of opportunities for inter-school networking, other than the exam-related activities described above.

3.6.2 Keeping up with developments in the art world

Interviewees were also asked how they kept abreast of developments in the art world. Although there was no reference to it in the question, some interviewees from both CAP and randomly identified schools chose to focus on contemporary art practice in their answer. Responses reported below relate to the full sample of 54 interviewees.

Visits to galleries and, in a very few cases, to artists studios, were easily the most frequently cited means of keeping up to date with the changing art world (33 mentions). In four schools it was apparent that group visits by department staff were favoured, in two cases being undertaken as part of the CPD programme. Such collective experiences were seen to be more likely to generate valuable discussion.

> *I take staff off timetable once a year for this art conference and that is normally when we go to London and we go to particular art galleries. We do that normally the last two weeks of the summer term – that is our main way of looking to see what was going on.*
> Art teacher, randomly identified school

However, 15 of the sample referred to the shortage of time to visit galleries. While some believed that this should be enabled in working time, others indicated that the benefit to school derived from what they would do for their own interest in their own time. Ten references were made to the need for more information from galleries, or for it to be channelled more efficiently to teachers, either by a centralised emailing system, or through 'batching' information, possibly by regional offices of ACE.

Publications were cited by 19 interviewees as a source of current news, including the *Times Educational Supplement* (TES) and art magazines. One department benefited from a school library press clippings service. Three interviewees referred to the value of TV programmes ('Rolf Harris – bless him!').

Personal contacts and networking were referred to by 17 interviewees. Contacts included artists known to the interviewee from college days, artist's relatives, links with further education and higher education colleges, but only three local teachers' networks.

Internet websites were referred to by only three teachers in this part of the interview, although their responses to questions about particular modules makes it clear that the internet, as used both by teachers and pupils, was an important tool for keeping abreast of developments.

3.6.3 Teacher identified factors influencing their choices of artist, art genres and images to include as curriculum content

Interviewees were also asked directly what influenced their choice of art genres, artists or images for inclusion in the curriculum they delivered, thus focusing more on the positive choice rather than the negative inhibitors to choosing.

Their responses were coded, resulting in the following classification.

Personal preference was easily the most frequently cited factor, with 25 interviewees acknowledging the significance of what they liked, what excited them and what they were familiar with in their choosing.

> *Personal taste, artists that you like and admire.*
> Art teacher, randomly identified school

> *You get to follow your own interest then and I think that makes it more interesting for the teacher as opposed to following something prescribed. I don't like prescribed schemes of work – I think you should work to your own interest.*
> Art teacher, randomly identified school

> *…to be honest, I don't like surrealism that much so I tend not to use it.*
> Art teacher, randomly identified school

> *Stuff that I like. I've got to enjoy it myself. With GCSE, the books are all mine, I buy them. I spend my money on them so I kind of like them and the kids know that it's a biased choice of books.*
> Head of department, CAP identified school

One teacher expressed some unease at the realisation that personal preference drove the choice of images, and one interviewee challenged the validity of a teacher's personal taste being a valid basis on which to make content decisions.

Unfortunately, this latter view was not elaborated.

> *Things that I like, which shouldn't be the right answer, but things I like and inspire me I think will inspire them. Just things I like or inspire me. I think I'm over enthusiastic sometimes and kids go, 'Oh yes!', but, like smiles, it's infectious.*
Art teacher, CAP identified school

> *It's certainly not whether I like them or not – it has been in the past.*
Head of department, CAP identified school

Department influence as a factor has already been addressed. The tendency of some departments to discuss preferences and share images, the encouragement from heads of department to build modules to suit individual skills and needs, and the extent to which written modules are prescriptive of content were all seen as playing their part.

Project relevance was cited by 16 interviewees, but presumably taken as read by other interviewees. However, the meaning of 'project relevance' within this category varied considerably. One teacher clearly had a predetermined match of particular artists to particular purposes, while another sought examples to illustrate techniques or ideas.

> *If we are outdoors we will be looking at Monet and the pointillists. If we are thinking about movement it will be the futurists. Certain artists are obviously wonderful educational tools. For example, Picasso covers basic elements, concepts, emotional aspects and the range of his work is wonderful. Certain images are universal – Degas's and Matisse's dancers are popular, especially with the girls. The Turner Prize lot and conceptual art is useful for thinking about how art needs to be relevant.*
Art teacher, randomly identified school

> *There are two ways we make decisions about which sort of art we use. The first is technique, and the second is a similar sort of idea, a similar sort of image that the artists has made, and is it relevant, is there a link, is there a connection?*
Art teacher, randomly identified school

Accessibility of images for pupils was cited by 14 interviewees as a factor in choosing art images. Here, the range of reasoning could be very wide indeed. In five cases the interviewee referred to the need to choose images that pupils could understand, that were not too complicated or too conceptual. Others referred to the desire to challenge pupils or to 'getting them thinking'.

> *I think I look at it from their point of view. I think they're so used to seeing Van Gogh and Monet and artists like that ... I wanted to do a quite contemporary artist and show that kind of aspect of it. And from looking at all the leaflets they've designed, they really enjoyed looking at something quite different. It really challenged them.*
> Art teacher, randomly identified school

> *We try to make sure they have some understanding of the most famous artists to start with and then contrast that with people who are more unusual to give them some idea of the choices they have in art. I think the whole thing is getting them thinking for themselves and realising that they can make leaps of the imagination in art. There's a lot about lateral thinking as well, and getting them to see that artists have done this, and that they can do it themselves.*
> Head of department, CAP identified school

One statement seems to sum up the way teachers steer between that which is too familiar, and that which is too challenging.

> *Something different that they've never done before, but also nothing that will scare them off.*
> Head of department, CAP identified school

It is not apparent from the data why there should be such differing views on what pupils can assimilate by way of challenging material. There are no obvious differences concerning the catchments of the schools concerned or the local art resources. Once more, the perspectives of the individual teacher, informed to some extent by the department approach, seem to be the main determinant.

Availability of resources, or lack of resources, was seen by nine teachers as a factor in their choice of art images. While virtually any image is available, the ability to reproduce enough copies for classroom use, and the size of images available, could determine whether an image was included. External sources were seen to be an influential factor by 18 interviewees, with all citing gallery exhibitions in this category, and seven referring to sources such as the internet, magazines and books. One referred to the valuable injection of new ideas for images made by initial teacher education students on placement.

3.7 Teacher responses to a selection of art images

Further insights concerning the way art images were chosen as curriculum content were gained from a more experimental research exercise. This involved showing teachers a set of six images and seeking their responses to them (the images are shown in Appendix 2).

- Image 1, a work of digital art by a school pupil (cropped to conceal the identity of the artist), was selected from the Chrisi Bailey Awards website. It is in collage form, and depicts the artist's view of himself in his environment.

- Image 2, by David Shrigley, contains the handwritten headline, 'TERRIBLE NEWS', followed by the words, in small letters, 'NO MORE TREATS'.

- Image 3 is Richard Billingham's untitled photograph of his parents kissing on a folding chair in their lounge.

- Image 4 is Van Gogh's *Bedroom*.

- Image 5 is a photograph of Damien Hirst's *The physical impossibility of death in the mind of someone living* (1991), the shark in a tank.

- Image 6 is Andy Warhol's multiple image *Marilyn x 100* (1962).

This list was not representative and it is acknowledged that there were limitations in the selection.

Interviewees were shown the images one at a time, in the above order and asked the following open questions: 'Is this an image you would consider using in your art lessons?', 'Why, or why not?' After responding to each of the images in turn, interviewees were asked which they would be most likely, and least likely to use. The exercise was conducted with no prior warning, and teachers interviewed first were asked not to raise the issue with colleagues yet to be interviewed. It should be said that the selection was intended to be somewhat provocative, and sought instant responses. Any findings are presented with the following caveats.

- The juxtaposition of images may well have affected responses.

- A more considered appraisal of the images, such as might apply in the normal lesson planning process, might have elicited different responses.

- Responses as part of a research process might be different from real situation responses.

- Some element of researcher judgement was occasionally needed to classify responses.

For these reasons, what follows is offered as an indication of attitudes to art images as part of curriculum content rather than as firm findings about how teachers choose art images.

Of the full sample, the process of responding to the images was undertaken by 29 class teachers and seven heads of department. (Because of the considerable time and commitment being asked of interviewees, especially heads of department, it was agreed that the response to images section would only be included if time permitted.)

Teacher reactions were grouped as follows, with multiple responses being possible for any one image. The responses are categorised under a descriptive coding that emerged from the discourse of the teachers rather than from a pre-determined classification.

Positive verdict. Respondents answering 'yes' were already using, or would consider using, the image in art lessons. (Where answers were equivocal to the point of balance, or if the teacher identified some educational potential, it was counted as a 'yes').

Teacher expression of personal reaction – teachers responded by expressing their own personal reaction to the image, divided into positive and negative.

Teacher expression of their prediction of pupil reaction – again divided into positive and negative.

Example to pupils – teachers expressed their view on the image as an example to pupils, without reference to any particular aspect of art learning. These were divided into good and bad examples.

Example of genre – teachers referred to the potential of the image to illustrate or represent a particular genre.

Content/issue – teachers referred to the potential of the image to lead to consideration or discussion of meaning, content or issues in the image.

Question of art – teachers referred to the potential of the image to stimulate a consideration of the question, 'What is art?'

Skills – teachers referred to the potential of the image to support the learning of particular art skill(s).

Over-exposure – teachers referred to the extent to which the image is at risk of becoming overused.

A simple count of the responses indicated the various ways in which teachers perceive the value of each of the images as contributors to visual art learning. Table 3.2 indicates the frequency of citations for each image under each type of response.

Table 3.2 Responses of art teachers to a selection of images of art works

Response type	Image 1 Pupil's digital image	Image 2 Terrible News	Image 3 Parents Kissing	Image 4 Bedroom	Image 5 Shark	Image 6 Marilyn
Positive verdict	33	16	24	30	30	34
Teacher positive reaction	–	1	5	1	–	–
Teacher negative reaction	2	12	7	8	1	6
Teacher prediction of positive pupil reaction	3	–	2	5	13	6
Teacher prediction of negative pupil reaction	–	4	10	–	1	–
Good example	5	3	–	2	–	–
Bad example	3	13	–	–	–	–
Genre	11	1	–	–	1	16
Content/issue	9	10	19	7	7	11
Question of art	–	6	2	–	14	–
Skills	29	8 (3neg)	10	26	12	26
Over-exposure	–	–	–	7	–	4
Image most likely to be used	5	3	5	7	3	18
Image least likely to be used	1	17	5	5	2	0

Note: Responses in the final two rows do not total to 36. A few teachers chose more than one most likely, and four did not identify a 'least likely to use' image.
Source: NFER interviews with art teachers and heads of department, 2003/4, n = 36.

Notwithstanding the caveats listed earlier, the exercise perhaps gives some indications concerning the way teachers choose images of art as part of their curriculum content.

Warhol's *Marilyn x 100* was identified by all interviewees as an image that they would use in their teaching, although four expressed some concern that it was overused as an image.

> *Everyone knows this one. It's starting to get a bit like the Van Gogh one, it's starting to get a bit overused, but it's good for prints.*
> Art teacher, randomly identified school

> *Good old Andy Warhol – right across the board. I'm a bit fed up with pop art, but we can't get away with not using it – everyone loves it.*
> Art teacher CAP identified school

Even though they were still using it, several teachers described the piece as 'boring', suggesting that choosing art that reflected their own interests was not always the paramount consideration – certain images seem to be included as of right. There were also references to the appeal that this type of image has for pupils.

> *It is a very good example of an everyday image, or one of that time, that has been used and is still used today, but it is really good and they love it, all kids love it.*
> Art teacher, randomly identified school

This was also the image most likely to be associated with an art genre, pop art being frequently addressed as a module in school art. It also scored very highly as useful in illustrating particular skills that pupils would need to develop. *Marilyn* also scored highly in terms of references to the content or issues associated with the work. These included concepts of stardom and art as part of consumerism.

> *The more able will understand the concept of repeating a very commercial image, even though it's a person. The less able will use it for its simplicity and the way it's been produced, but they won't necessarily go for the meaning behind it.*
> Art teacher, randomly identified school

The pupil's digital image ran a close second as includable in the curriculum content, even though this would have been the first viewing of the work by most interviewees, but like *Marilyn*, it elicited no expressions of personal appeal from teachers.

> *It's pretty modern – they could make a collage on contemporary culture.*
> Art teacher, randomly identified school

> *I'd look at the colours, what it said about this kid. Why is it…does it look like he is trapped, is that a car mirror?*
> Art teacher, CAP identified school

> *I like the fact that it was done by a pupil. A lot of the art they are doing at school is about personal interests and things that represent themselves, so this is a good example of that.*
> Head of department, randomly identified school

> *I think it's a lovely one for pupils to try and work out the meaning of.*
> Head of department, CAP identified school

It was also frequently referred to as valuable, as an example of a particular genre. This image was also favoured because it illustrated particular skills (collage, digital manipulation, pattern, photomontage and graphics) that were high on teacher priorities. It was also favoured because it provided an example of what young people could achieve, and was thought to be especially appealing to boys, though whether this was because of its content or form is not clear.

> *An example like that would be very good – particularly for the lads, who would prefer that to a painting.*
> Art teacher, CAP identified school

It was also felt by several respondents that aspects of the content of the image – environment, personal identity and modern culture – were of value to pupils.

Van Gogh's *Bedroom* elicited a polarised response. It was both admired as curriculum content and dismissed as badly over-used and boring.

> *I think the style of painting would be quite interesting for them to look at, but other than that I don't really like it as a piece of work and just personally, it doesn't inspire me that much… I don't think it's something I would choose to do.*
> Art teacher, randomly identified school

Again, its capacity to illustrate particular skills was welcomed, but it was one of the least cited in terms of its content. It is notable that although 30 interviewees said they do or would use this image, five identified it as the one they would be least likely to use, totalling more than the sample size. This would appear to be a protest vote against the over-use of the image.

Hirst's *The physical impossibility of death in the mind of someone living*, or rather the photograph of the work, also scored highly as an image that would be included in the curriculum, but here the reasons were somewhat diverse. It had the highest score as likely to appeal to pupils, either because they knew of Hirst's reputation and were intrigued by it, or perhaps because of a morbid fascination with dead animals.

> *You can use a lot of examples to create a talking point before a project. 'What's that?' 'It's sick. It's weird, it's strange.' The lads all think it's brilliant, the girls all go 'Yuch!' That's sexist, but that's what happens. 'Could you call it surreal?' As talking points, yes.*
> Art teacher, randomly identified school

This image was deemed especially valuable for raising the question 'What is art?' but had surprisingly few references to the content or issues raised by the image. Skills were not mentioned frequently, and when they were, they were mentioned not so much as examples for pupils to emulate but rather to wonder at. Two interviewees rejected the image because they felt that a photograph could not do justice to the impact of the installation itself.

> *Pupils like his work, but I'd probably be less likely to use this one than some of the others because the flat image doesn't do it justice – to understand it you need to see the whole thing, to walk around it.*
> Art teacher, randomly identified school

Billingham's photograph of his parents kissing scored relatively low as an image that would be included in the curriculum. It elicited perhaps the most polarised response of all the images. Teachers tended to either like it or loathe it, and also to think their pupils would either relate to it, or reject it.

> *It's a fabulous image.*
> *For me personally, I just don't find it an exciting enough image.*
> Two art teachers from the same randomly identified school

I wouldn't use this one. Teenage girls would be stupid if they saw it, they'd laugh. They'd just think, 'It's crap!' I personally find that really uninteresting – I'd find it really hard to justify that.
Art teacher, CAP identified school

This one would not work in America but over here everyone seems much more open to sexuality in schools. I probably personally wouldn't use this one – it brings up all kinds of issues that I wouldn't want to discuss when there'd be other images I could use.
Art teacher, randomly identified school

They'd like to look at that one, and it would quite amuse them, but it doesn't fit in with any of our schemes of work and I'd be quite concerned that it'd look like some of their front rooms.
Head of department, randomly identified school

Yes, I'd use it with all years. Especially for year 8, people within their environment. They'd quite like it and then we could have a great discussion about the faces on the wall or home décor – would you like a room like this?
Art teacher, randomly identified school

The teachers' personal responses usually linked to the content, but in a few cases referred to the quality of the photographic composition. Where skills were referred to, these were usually related to portraiture or composition. Their prediction of pupil response most frequently referred to the likelihood that the image would promote a 'silly' reaction leading to poor behaviour, especially amongst key stage 3 pupils. However, this image was most likely to elicit comments concerning the content and issues raised. Some felt that the image was too close for comfort for their pupils, while others felt that they would relate well to seeing a depiction of life as they knew it to be.

It's too controversial for the lower school – it could stir up a lot of issues as they could relate it to their own homes.
Art teacher, randomly identified school

That image is likely to repulse them. Old people don't have sex, and fat people definitely don't have sex. Girls in this school wouldn't be able to relate to the image or really understand its context.
Art teacher, randomly identified school

The issues most frequently mentioned were relationships, the environment, poverty, emotions and self.

> *We do portraits and self-image, and that could open up a discussion about social issues.*
> Art teacher, randomly identified school, same as previous quote

> *Things like this are lovely. When you try to get them to do things on relationships or emotions they don't look at real emotions. This would definitely cause giggling but would be excellent for discussion. I think the older ones would be able to take the notion of intruding on someone on board and think about the context.*
> Head of department, CAP identified school

> *They love the dirty, crude images. It's more exciting to them than Van Gogh.*
> Head of department, CAP identified school

It would appear that the polarisation of reactions was in part related to the school context, to the idea that such an image would be either too familiar or too alien to pupils. However, teachers in the same school could have profoundly differing views on the image, suggesting that personal response was a powerful determinant of usage.

David Shrigley's *Terrible news – no more treats* was the least likely to be included in the curriculum by some distance. This image was located in the Digital Art Resource for Education (DARE) website as an example of contemporary art, but appeared to be unknown to any interviewees. Many teachers reacted against it themselves, and some thought that pupils would also reject it, suggesting that they would not understand it or think it childish.

> *I just can't imagine what the pupils would think of it. They wouldn't understand it.*
> Art teacher, randomly identified school

> *Probably not. I just think the writing is horrible, and it wouldn't inspire me.*
> Art teacher, randomly identified school

> *Badly written, badly presented. I don't think it's offering anything to the kids. I don't think they'd gain anything from that.*
> Art teacher, randomly identified school

When you teach children, you have to try and encourage them to develop their skills more. If I gave them that, they would just look at me like I was mad. It wouldn't encourage them to get the skills that they'd need for GCSE.
Head of department, randomly identified school

While several thought it would be a bad example to show to pupils, some thought it might encourage those of lesser ability to try, if they realised that work displaying this level of technical skills could also be regarded as art, valued for its meaning rather than its technical finesse. Some teachers felt that the image could generate debate about the meaning of the image and the nature of art.

It's a good example to show students that you don't have to do a fantastic painting for it to be art – it's about making a statement. This piece would work well in an issue-based module.
Art teacher, CAP identified school

It fits in with a year 9 project. I would use it as a starting point – what does it mean? What ideas come out of it? What are treats? What is terrible news?
Head of department, CAP identified school

Some overarching observations

The reactions of teachers raise a number of issues concerning the selection of art images for inclusion as curriculum content.

It is notable that, consistent with a dominant theme presented throughout Chapters 2 and 3, the relevance of the images as a whole to the teaching of skills is the most frequently raised response. The possibility of including an image with skills apparently below the level of pupils is seen by some to be potentially damaging. (Researchers regretted not including an 'old master' as an example of what might conventionally be seen as very high technical skills in order to assess the reaction.)

It would appear that the issue of acceptability emerged as important. Thus, an image showing insufficient apparent skills (*Terrible News*) was more likely not to find a place in the curriculum, as was an image that might provoke a problematic reaction (parents kissing). It was notable that a dead animal would be very acceptable compared to a show of affection between adults; this in spite of the fact that parents kissing was seen as potentially useful for raising issues of content. However, the acceptability and educational value of Van Gogh's *Bedroom* for most interviewees outweighed the view that it was boring or over-exposed.

Similarly, while Hirst's shark was seen as a good opportunity to examine what constitutes art, *Terrible News* was perhaps seen as so unacceptable that it was much less likely to be considered in that context. The latter also scored fairly highly as likely to raise issues about its content, but this in itself failed to increase its popularity or acceptability greatly.

3.7.1 Differences between teachers from CAP and randomly identified schools

The scoring exercise was conducted 'blind' to the identities of the interviewees in order to avoid bias in coding. By chance, an equal number of teachers from both contemporary and random schools were asked the questions concerning the images. Researchers sought to ascertain whether there was a significant difference in the responses of teachers in CAP identified schools and randomly identified schools. For the most part, there was little evidence to indicate that the reactions of teachers in the two cohorts of schools varied greatly. For example, there was no significant difference between the two cohorts in expressing their personal attitudes to the two least popular images, parents kissing and *Terrible News*. Similarly, the negative reaction to the Van Gogh picture was shared by the two cohorts.

Only one substantial numerical difference between the responses of the two cohorts could be identified. Teachers from CAP identified schools provided a total of 26 citations of ways in which the six images could be used to address issues and matters of content. Teachers from randomly identified schools offered 37 such citations. Researchers were not able to identify any reason for this discrepancy. However, the highest scores by teachers in randomly identified schools for content were for Image 1 (digital art by school pupil) and Image 6 (Warhols' *Marilyn*), for which teachers in CAP schools made few citations concerning content or issues. Teachers in randomly identified schools, unlike those in CAP identified schools, also cited Hirst's shark frequently in this respect. In each of these three cases it might be argued that the content and issues aspects were more conventionally acceptable, compared to the still controversial aspect of parents kissing, and the challenge to artistic excellence in *Terrible News*. Some teachers may have been looking for a justification to include *Terrible News* in spite of what they saw as the absence of artistic merit. An alternative possibility may be that teachers in CAP schools had taken as read the content element of some of the images and felt no need to refer to it.

There appears to be some evidence of a slow-changing orthodoxy in the selection of art images to include in the curriculum. While some images (Van Gogh's *Bedroom* and Warhol's *Marilyn*) remain part of the canon, they are perhaps under threat. Other images, such as *Terrible News* and parents kissing are less likely to enter the canon at present, either because they are not perceived as art of sufficient quality or because they might be too challenging to address with children. On the other hand, an item such as Hirst's shark does appear to have already attained approval, perhaps at least in part because it has already achieved some fame or notoriety. As well as teacher appeal, predicted pupil appeal appears to be one of the determinants concerning the inclusion of particular images.

3.8 Summary and conclusions

It might be claimed that, given the massive potential range of artists and art images available for inclusion in the curriculum for school art, the actual choices made are somewhat limited. This research was able to suggest and provide evidence for a number of factors that influence the choices made.

National or school-level contextual issues

Neither the National Curriculum nor the QCA guidelines were experienced as restrictive by the considerable majority of interviewees. However, there were those expressing concern that the GCSE syllabuses might limit the opportunity to excel, especially for more able pupils. The primacy of skills in the assessment process was apparent, but not regarded by teachers as restrictive.

The ethos of individual schools was not seen to limit curriculum choices, but several interviewees did refer to the cultural poverty of their pupils and how this limited what pupils could assimilate.

Decisions and guidelines by school art departments were generally seen as enabling, to the extent that heads of department were generally very supportive of teachers choosing curriculum content to suit their own interests and skills.

However, few departments had policy documents setting out the philosophy of art learning and teaching, restricting themselves usually to the more prosaic aspects of planning and curriculum foci.

Both department documentation and interviewee discourse revealed a very prevalent orthodoxy that the teaching of art skills at key stage 3 should precede a move towards more exploratory and independent learning at key stage 4.

There was a discernible tendency amongst heads of department in CAP identified schools to focus more on pupil experience, the importance of ideas, current events and external stimuli (such as gallery exhibitions).

However, less than a third of interviewees were of the definite opinion that their curriculum adequately reflected current developments in the art world, with some questioning whether it could or even should.

Resource issues

A number of specific resource factors were perceived to inhibit curriculum content choices, namely space, the availability of materials, art images or computers, access to galleries and/or artist studios and time. Of these, space was the most widely cited inhibitor, affecting teachers in CAP and randomly identified schools equally.

However, teachers in randomly identified schools were more than twice as likely to cite resource shortages as an inhibitor, and almost twice as likely to cite shortage of time as an inhibitor. One might question whether that is the result of actual difference in the time or resources available, or a difference in attitude between the two cohorts of teachers.

Teacher-specific issues

Differences in the training backgrounds of the two cohorts were also evident, with teachers in CAP identified schools being more likely to have a fine art degree. Of the 23 teachers in the overall sample with other degrees, ten were in fashion or textiles, six in graphic or other design and three in ceramics. Heads of departments were more likely to have fine art degrees than class teachers. References were made in interviews to the need for teachers to share their expertise and knowledge, and the only individuals specifically identified by other teachers as sources of artistic references were those with fine art degrees.

Staff in CAP identified schools were more likely to have worked as professional artists before entering teaching, and thus may be able to share a more thorough understanding of the art production process with their pupils.

There appeared to be a dearth of courses in art or art teaching for practising teachers. Courses related to GCSE examinations, especially concerning assessment, comprised the majority of CPD opportunities both for teachers and heads of departments.

Issues relating to keeping abreast of art developments

References were made in interviews to the need for teachers to share their knowledge of artists, genres and examples, either through teacher networks or within department teams.

Courses run by galleries were more likely to be referred to by heads of departments than by art teachers. Visits to galleries were easily the most frequently cited means of keeping up with developments in the art world, but a significant number of interviewees referred to the shortage of time to visit galleries.

Other means of keeping up with the changing art world were publications followed by personal contacts or networks.

Issues relating to teacher attitudes to art images

Asked directly what influenced their choice of images for inclusion as curriculum content, personal preference was easily the most frequently cited factor. The accessibility of images to pupils was frequently cited, features including attractiveness and the need to be understandable and not too conceptual. Others referred to the desire to challenge pupils or to 'get them thinking'.

When responding to a set of six specific images, it became very clear that the capacity of an image to support the learning of art form skills was very important. Images less relevant to skill learning, even if they elicited more comments concerning their value in terms of content and meaning, were less likely to be included in the curriculum.

An image raising potentially embarrassing or personally challenging issues was less likely to be included than an image thought to offer opportunities for skills teaching, even though it was regarded by many as boring or over-exposed.

While a famous art installation was regarded as valuable as a focus for discussing 'What is art?', a lesser known but acknowledged text-based item, apparently displaying a low skills level, was not.

Perhaps curiously, teachers from randomly identified schools were more likely to cite the meaning and issues in images than were their colleagues in CAP identified schools. The reason for this is unclear. One hypothesis is that teachers in randomly identified schools felt a greater need to justify an image that they might otherwise have to reject on the basis of limited artistic value.

Finally, there appeared to be evidence of a slow-changing orthodoxy in the choice of curriculum content, with some teachers continuing to include certain images even though they saw them as boring or over-exposed.

We have explored the various factors that might influence the content of the secondary school art curriculum in this chapter. Chapter 4 addresses the perceived value of the art curriculum and the particular contribution that contemporary art practice might make to it.

Questions for policy makers and practitioners

- How would a change to a more even balance between the teaching of skills and addressing issues and meaning in art, lead to a different selection of references and media?
- Is there evidence that enabling teachers to develop as practising artists (as is being addressed by the Artist Teacher Scheme) might result in a broader or more effective art education for school pupils?
- Should personal preference be a criterion for the selection of art images to include in the school art curriculum?
- To what extent can contemporary art be intellectually accessible to pupils?
- Would the greater prioritisation of issues and meaning in art, often claimed to be enabled by the inclusion of contemporary art practice, deter pupils from choosing art as an option at GCSE?

4 The perceived impact of contemporary art practice in the secondary school art curriculum

4.1 Introduction

The literature review conducted in the first phase of this study revealed a substantial amount of existing research concerned with the impact and effects derived from the study of art in general. This chapter focuses on the perceived impact on pupils of programmes including contemporary art practice, based on the perspectives of teachers interviewed in the CAP identified schools.

To put this into context, the chapter first explores the perceived value of the art curriculum as a whole, as described by teachers both in randomly and CAP identified schools (section 4.2)

Section 4.3 considers the reasons cited by teachers in CAP identified schools for including contemporary art practice in the school art curriculum. It then goes on to consider the perceived learning effects and outcomes of programmes including contemporary art practice.

References are made to the perceptions of the 13 pupils who were interviewed in those CAP identified schools where an extended visit took place.

The chapter concludes with a summary of the findings (section 4.4).

4.2 The perceived outcomes of the art curriculum

Teachers in the full sample of schools were asked, 'What is your perception of what the students gain from the art curriculum delivered here?', and were asked to elaborate on any perceived contributions to wider learning. Previous work by Harland *et al.* (2000) discussed in the literature review, proposed a typology of pupil effects derived from the arts in secondary schools. This comprised seven types of effects, as follows:

- **intrinsic and immediate effects: forms of enjoyment and therapy:** the immediate effects of participating in arts activities, including personal enjoyment, fulfilment or an increased sense of wellbeing

- **art form knowledge and skills:** knowledge, understanding and appreciation of the arts (including interpretative skills for judgement making), as well as the development of technical skills and capabilities in an art form.

- **knowledge in the social and cultural domain:** Knowledge of the cultural domain (a greater awareness of cultural traditions and multicultural perspectives), enhancements in pupils' awareness of their surroundings (environmental contexts) and developments in pupils' understanding of social and moral issues.

- **creativity and thinking skills**: The acquisition of thinking and problem-solving skills and the development of creativity, imagination and the ability to innovate.

- **communication and expressive skills:** Interactive communication skills (language development and listening skills), increased pupil confidence to express themselves and the capacity to use the arts as a tool of expression.

- **personal and social development:** The development of a sense of self, enhanced self-esteem and self-confidence, enhanced social skills and an awareness of others (empathy).

- **extrinsic transfer effects:** Effects which can be carried over or transferred from the immediate context of the arts lesson, for example, into other curriculum areas of the world of work and employment.

The responses of the full sample of teachers in this research was analysed and it emerged that their perspectives of the effects of the visual art curriculum as delivered in their schools accorded with the above typology. Table 4.1 sets out the number of citations by teachers in both the CAP and the randomly identified schools against each of the effects.

Percentages are given in order to draw comparisons between the two cohorts. It is worth noting that the overall numbers are small and that any differences between the actual numbers of interviewees reporting each effect in both cohorts are limited.

These perceptions of the effects of the art curriculum are based on responses to an open question and interviewees were not asked specifically about each type of effect. Thus, the outcomes identified are those that teachers chose to highlight.

Table 4.1 The perceived impacts derived from the art curriculum

Effects of art education	Percentage of teachers in CAP identified schools citing effect (number)	Percentage of teachers in random schools citing effect (number)	Percentage of all teachers (number)
Intrinsic and immediate effects: forms of enjoyment and therapy	21 (5)	13 (4)	17 (9)
Art form knowledge and skills	50 (12)	33 (10)	41 (22)
Knowledge in the social and cultural domain	29 (7)	33 (10)	31 (17)
Creativity and thinking skills	25 (6)	23 (7)	24 (13)
Communication and expressive skills	21 (5)	10 (3)	15 (8)
Personal and social development	29 (7)	30 (9)	30 (16)
Extrinsic transfer effects	29 (7)	30 (9)	30 (16)

N = CAP identified school 24 interviewees, randomly identified schools 30 interviewees.
Most teachers cited more than one impact, thus the categories are not mutually exclusive and the percentages can sum up to more than 100 per cent.
Source: NFER interviews conducted with art teachers and heads of art departments (2003/2004)

In considering these responses one might assume that certain outcomes are so inevitable from the teaching of art that they do not need mentioning. For example, one might assume that all teachers would see the acquisition of art form knowledge and skills as an outcome of the art curriculum. It is also possible that certain outcomes, whilst prevalent, were not accorded as much value as others by the teachers in the sample and thus did not emerge through interview.

Intrinsic and immediate effects: forms of enjoyment and therapy

This first category includes references to enjoyment, satisfaction and 'light relief' from the perceived academic exertion of other subject areas. Impacts associated with this category were mentioned by nine (17 per cent) of the teachers interviewed in this research.

In addition, three pupils commented that their art lessons provided them with a sense of achievement, primarily derived from the satisfaction of completing a piece of art that they were pleased with. A further three pupils said that they derived enjoyment from their art lessons.

> *I think the idea of an art lesson for me is an enjoyable time, partly because I enjoy art and partly because in the lessons we really are encouraged to do what we want to do and that makes it very enjoyable.*
>
> Pupil, CAP identified school

Art form knowledge and skills

A combined total of 22 teachers (41 per cent) cited the development of art form knowledge and skills, making this the most frequently cited effect. However, whilst a high proportion of interviewees reported this type of outcome, over half did not. As discussed, this may have resulted from an assumption that the acquisition of art form knowledge and skills is so fundamental to the teaching of art that it did not need highlighting.

Art form skills

The acquisition of art form skills (observational drawing, using materials and techniques, formal elements) was cited more frequently than the acquisition of art form knowledge for both cohorts. However, more teachers in CAP identified schools stated that the curriculum contributed to the development of such skills than their colleagues in the randomly identified schools (nine teachers compared to five), perhaps suggesting that those teachers felt the need to assert their commitment to skill teaching even though they pursued other agendas as well.

> *We really do value traditional skills – we have to make sure we can use skills through contemporary art and not use contemporary art which doesn't necessarily exploit traditional skills.*
>
> Art teacher, CAP identified school

The clear majority (11 of the 13 pupils interviewed) also felt that they gained increased art form skills.

Art form knowledge

Five teachers (17 per cent) in the randomly identified schools and 7 (29 per cent) in the CAP identified schools, felt the curriculum they taught contributed to pupils' knowledge and appreciation of art in the wider world. However, teachers in the CAP identified schools frequently highlighted the belief that the inclusion of contemporary art in the curriculum played a key role in providing pupils with a wider overview of artists and genres. Data in Chapters 2 and 3 clearly indicates a discrepancy between the two cohorts of teachers concerning the range of art to which they expose their pupils. Whether a greater volume and range of art references generates greater art form knowledge is arguable – a smaller frame of reference may support more in-depth knowledge, while a larger frame may be seen to increase the menu of choices available to pupils.

Five pupil interviewees cited an increased awareness and appreciation of art, artists and artistic genres as a result of the art curriculum that they received.

Knowledge in the social and cultural domain

A combined total of 17 teachers (31 per cent) referred to impacts under this category, including cultural awareness and the exploration of issues.

> *They are able to deal with the issues that surround them in today's world – able to approach the complexities of modern life with an attitude which is not convergent but divergent.*
> Art teacher, CAP identified school

The National Curriculum for art and design states that: 'The study of art and design can contribute to an understanding of spiritual, ethical, social and citizenship issues' (QCA, 2003c, p.1). However, only a third of interviewees (from both cohorts of schools) highlighted outcomes of this nature, suggesting perhaps that teachers do not prioritise or consider this aspect of the curriculum as much as the acquisition of art form skills.

Creativity and thinking skills

A total of 13 teachers (24 per cent) cited the development of creativity and thinking skills, which included the subcategories of lateral thinking skills and developed imagination and creativity.

Lateral thinking skills

Six (25 per cent) of the teachers in the CAP identified schools cited the development of lateral thinking skills, such as problem solving and decision making, compared to three (10 per cent) of their colleagues in the randomly identified schools. This is perhaps indicative of a curriculum in these schools that is more likely to encourage lateral thinking through experimentation and conceptual approaches to making art. As outlined in Chapter 2, teachers in the CAP identified schools were more likely to highlight the development of creative thinking skills by their pupils in their module descriptions.

Developed imagination and creativity

Ten teachers (five from each cohort of schools) claimed the development of imagination and creativity as an impact of the art curriculum for pupils. The development of these capabilities was primarily cited as evident in the work the pupils produced in art lessons and the processes they undertook to generate their ideas.

> *It's to do with the thought processes they* [the pupils] *use; it* [art] *makes you think outside the box and it makes you think in different ways, more creatively, more inventively and more imaginatively.*
> Head of department, CAP identified school

However, imagination and creativity were also seen as transferable skills, of benefit to the rest of the pupils' studies.

> *Just because you are doing maths or science doesn't mean you can't think creatively.*
> Head of department, randomly identified school

Communication and expressive skills

A total of eight teachers (15 per cent) felt that the art curriculum generated increased communication and expressive skills in pupils. Examples of this group of skills included the ways in which pupils were better able to use art as a visual communication tool, and their increased ability to express their opinion both on the art works they study and the issues and concepts within these.

> *They are invited to express their opinions about certain things more than they would be in other subjects.*
> Art teacher, randomly identified school

This group of skills was cited as an outcome by three (10 per cent) of the teachers in random schools and five (21 per cent) of the teachers in CAP identified schools. As highlighted in Chapter 2, expression of meaning was identified as a taught skill in 18 per cent of the modules in CAP identified schools compared to just 6 per cent of the modules in randomly identified schools.

Four pupils cited increased communication skills and the ability to express themselves through their art.

> *You need to learn how to express yourself, otherwise if something bad happens you won't be able to let it out. If I was in an angry mood I could sit there and*

draw something and feel better.
Pupil, CAP identified school

Personal and social development

Personal and social development was cited as an impact derived from the art curriculum by 16 teachers (30 per cent).

Personal development

The most commonly cited area of personal development was increased confidence. Ten teachers (five from each cohort of schools) suggested that pupils gained confidence as a result of their art lessons. Primarily, this increase in confidence was seen as a result of being able to achieve in art, particularly for lower ability or less academic pupils, who may not be deriving a sense of achievement from other subject areas. Group discussions (expressing an opinion and being listened to), putting pupils' work on display and allowing pupils the independence to experiment with materials and ideas without criticising the outcome were all cited as additional ways in which art lessons contributed to confidence building.

One teacher described the approach used in her art department, which focused on recognising the positive achievements of the pupils, and the way in which this contributes to their personal development and subsequent engagement with the art curriculum.

> *Working in this way opens doors for the pupils. It's about starting here and seeing what happens and not building in possibilities for failure. Once you build in a hurdle that is too hard to climb, unnecessarily, you get a lack of confidence and all interest has gone.*
> Art teacher, CAP identified school

Five pupils cited an increase in their confidence resulting from their art education. This increased confidence primarily related to the confidence to express their opinions, and was associated with an increased respect for other opinions amongst their peer group, as a result of discussing art works or debating issues which arose.

> *It's about thinking more liberally, thinking in a more open way and being open to other people's work and other people's ideas.*
> Pupil, CAP identified school

Social development

Five teachers referred specifically to the development of pupils' social skills – one teacher in a randomly identified school and four teachers in CAP identified schools. Social skills included working with others, listening to and respecting others' opinions and working as a group to develop ideas.

> *At the beginning, when we first came up with our ideas, we were asked to share our ideas with the class and if we had a very vague idea then we'd explain it and we'd get help from the rest of the class ... that was helpful.*
> Pupil, CAP identified school

It may be that group art making, cited only in modules in CAP identified schools, contributed to the development of social skills.

Extrinsic transfer effects

A total of 16 teachers (30 per cent) referred to the development of transferable skills, primarily literacy, numeracy and research and evaluation skills. Research and evaluation skills ranked significantly lower than literacy and numeracy, and were cited by just four teachers overall. Research was taught as a distinct skill in just 10 per cent of the modules discussed, which may account for this, but investigating and researching as a thinking process featured in 92 per cent of the total modules (as discussed in Chapter 2). This raises the question as to why these skills are not more commonly cited as an outcome derived from the curriculum. It is possible that developing research skills is seen as so fundamental to the work being undertaken in the art curriculum that interviewees felt no need to mention it. But the data also suggests that research was often set as homework and not conducted under the direct supervision or instruction of teachers. Could there be an assumption amongst art teachers that pupil research skills are pre-existing, and are simply used in the art curriculum rather than taught or developed through it? If this were the case, it is possible that, while research outputs are expected of pupils, the teaching of research skills is relatively neglected. This may account for the frustration expressed by some teachers concerning the quality of research conducted by pupils.

The majority (11) of the pupils interviewed felt that they gained transferable skills from the art curriculum they received. Their responses included references to research, suggesting that, despite possible lack of articulation or recognition by teachers, pupils themselves saw increased research skills as a valuable transferable effect from studying art.

Four teachers cited pupils' improved career prospects as an impact derived from studying art. As well as equipping pupils with the skills needed to find careers in art-related disciplines (particularly design) two teachers also commented that the art curriculum increased pupils' general awareness of the further education and career possibilities associated with the subject.

4.3 The outcomes of art programmes that include contemporary art practice

The research sought to ascertain why some schools and teachers chose to include or accord a greater priority to contemporary practice in their art teaching. Although the research did not investigate the actual outcomes of the curriculum (in terms, for example, of pupil achievement), it also explored the perceptions of teachers concerning the particular additional contribution that the inclusion of contemporary art practice made to effects and learning outcomes of their art curriculum.

This section therefore explores the responses given by interviewees in the CAP identified schools to the following questions.

- Why do you choose to incorporate contemporary art practice in the curriculum?
- What are your perceptions of the learning effects and outcomes of programmes involving contemporary art?

Section 4.3.1 explores teachers' additional and specific intentions for incorporating contemporary art practice in their curriculum. Section 4.3.2 looks at any claims that contemporary art practice provides either additional contributions or enhancements to the more general effects of art education.

4.3.1 The reasons for the inclusion of contemporary art practice in the school art curriculum

Table 4.2 shows the reasons cited for the inclusion of contemporary art practice in the school art curriculum. Responses have not been classified in relation to any existing typology of aims, but are researcher classifications of the discourse of the interviewees. However, their relationship to the typology of effects set out in section 4.2 is explored in section 4.3.2.

Table 4.2 The reasons for choosing to incorporate contemporary art practice

The reasons for including contemporary art practice in the school art curriculum	Percentage of interviewees in CAP identified schools citing reason (number)
To provide a curriculum that is more interesting, relevant and accessible to the pupils	50 (12)
To increase pupils' understanding of the wider art world and challenge the notion of 'what is art?'	40 (9)
To incorporate individual teacher preference for contemporary genres	29 (7)
To encourage the development of thinking, questioning and conceptual thinking skills	21 (5)
To provide access to a wider range of media and materials and ways of working	16 (4)
To provide opportunities to explore the issues raised in contemporary pieces	13 (3)
To enable pupils to achieve in art (including good GCSE grades)	8 (2)

N = 24 interviewees. Most interviewees indicated more than one reason, thus the categories are not mutually exclusive and the percentages can sum up to more than 100 per cent.
Source: NFER interviews conducted with art teachers and heads of art departments in CAP identified schools (2003/2004)

To provide a curriculum that is more interesting, relevant and accessible to the pupils

The most common reason expressed for including contemporary art practice (cited by half of the interviewees in the CAP identified schools) was to ensure that the curriculum delivered contained material to which the pupils could relate, and with which they would be more engaged.

> *The best way to educate pupils is to have them on your side and contemporary art does that.*
Art teacher, CAP identified school

Contemporary art was seen as particularly engaging because of the content of contemporary images, and also because of the media in which it was produced.

> *They [the pupils] have the capacity now to think on different levels in different media, they do things in their homes, burn their own CDs and do animation on their home PCs. They are living in a multimedia culture, so I think they can access art like that more readily than understanding an abstract painting.*
Head of department, CAP identified school

Strongly opposing views emerged between interviewees, primarily, though not exclusively, between teachers in the two cohorts of schools, concerning the accessibility and perceived relevance of contemporary art for pupils. Whilst this was cited as the most common reason for its inclusion by teachers in the CAP identified schools, a greater tendency emerged amongst interviewees in the randomly identified schools to see contemporary art as inaccessible and alienating for pupils. This was primarily related to the content of much contemporary art and the perception that pupils in key stage 3 and 4 were not mature enough to understand the concepts presented, or that the issues might be too challenging to address in the classroom.

> *There is no point introducing conceptual art – they will just think it is a big joke. You have to start them off with images that will inspire them. If it's not pristine and neat they hate it and then you lose their attention and they don't succeed. If it's too conceptual and doesn't look like a beautiful piece of art work then they won't respond to it and that's when you get behavioural problems.*
> Head of department, randomly identified school

These polarised perspectives may indicate as much about the extent to which individual teachers themselves feel comfortable with contemporary art and the possible implications of incorporating it into the classroom, as about their view of its relevance to young people and their education. (See the analysis of interviewees' reactions to art images in Chapter 3 for more details.)

To increase pupils' understanding of the wider art world and challenge the notion of 'what is art?'

The second most frequently cited reason for the inclusion of contemporary art practice (cited by two-fifths of interviewees in the CAP identified schools) was the opportunities it was seen to provide to widen pupils' understanding and appreciation of art. In no schools in the sample were contemporary art references used to displace reference to other genres.

> *You can't just work on contemporary and skip the foundations of what's gone before.*
> Art teacher, CAP identified school

Instead, contemporary references were often used in addition to historical genres to increase the range of artistic references used to support the curriculum. In doing so, pupils had the opportunity to increase their knowledge of art forms, artists and genres.

> *Students' knowledge of artists is pretty limited so it's just as important to give them information about artists from 100 years ago – and cover Renaissance to Modernism – and then it is just as important to look at contemporary artists.*
> Art teacher, CAP identified school

In addition, exposure to, and discussion of controversial contemporary art, for example, installations such as Damien Hirst's *Away from the flock* or Tracey Emin's *My bed*, allowed teachers to challenge their pupils' preconceived ideas of the meaning and purpose of art.

To incorporate individual teacher preference for contemporary genres

Individual teacher preference emerged as the third most common reason for the inclusion of contemporary art practice, cited by approximately a third (29 per cent) of interviewees in the CAP identified schools. A number of interviewees commented that their work as a practising artist outside school, their recent art training or their general interest in the current art world all fed into a preference for contemporary genres. One reason for allowing personal preferences to influence the curriculum content focused on teacher motivation.

> *At the end of the day I go to art galleries. I see contemporary artists because I'm interested in them. So I don't want to be teaching something that I'm not stimulated by.*
> Art teacher, CAP identified school

The influence of individual teachers' skills, knowledge and personal preference and the impact of these on curriculum content was discussed previously in Chapter 3.

To encourage the development of thinking, questioning and conceptual thinking skills

The fourth reason cited for including contemporary art practice was to provide additional opportunities for pupils to develop the skills associated with looking at art (cited by five, 21 per cent, of the interviewees in the CAP identified schools). Examples of thinking, questioning and conceptual thinking skills included the skills of looking at a piece of art and discovering its meaning and the skills of researching and investigating the context of a piece of art in order to understand its significance. Some interviewees believed that contemporary art was well suited to this purpose. Teachers adopting this philosophy were more likely to see art as a medium through which they could educate pupils, rather than simply passing on art skills and knowledge.

> *I'm not here to create little artists. I'm here to educate through my subject.*
> Head of department, CAP identified school

The response from another interviewee outlined the relationship between this philosophy and the inclusion of contemporary art.

> *We are not training students to be artists, we are using art as a vehicle for questioning everything, a means to think in a very diverse way and contemporary art is the genre that leads us that way.*
> Head of department, CAP identified school

To provide access to a wider range of media and materials and ways of working

Four teachers (16 per cent) stated that they included contemporary art practice in the curriculum in order to provide pupils with access to a wide range of media, materials and ways of working. Contemporary art was seen as an appropriate arena for doing this, as contemporary references often provided stimuli for working in less traditional media. For example, digital images were used to inspire ICT-based projects.

To provide opportunities to explore the issues raised in contemporary pieces

Three teachers (13 per cent) felt that the content of much contemporary work provided a useful medium for the exploration of issues. It was noted that the issues raised in contemporary art were interesting and relevant to the pupils because they were about the society in which they lived, as opposed to historical contexts. Images that dealt with issues were used to make links with citizenship and to create a platform for discussion.

> *Contemporary artists are dealing with contemporary issues – it's more exciting to look at living artists and see what they are trying to say.*
> Art teacher, CAP identified school

Some teachers, primarily in the randomly identified schools, indicated that some aspects of contemporary art practice, and the issues raised through contemporary images, were too intellectually demanding or personally challenging for pupils.

However, those espousing contemporary art practice suggest that contemporary art images can provide useful opportunities to engage pupils intellectually in considering representations of issues to which they would feel some relationship.

To enable pupils to achieve in art (including good GCSE grades)

Lastly, two teachers (8 per cent) expressed the opinion that the inclusion of contemporary practices in the curriculum enabled more pupils to achieve in art, primarily by providing them with an art curriculum that did not focus solely on the development of skills and the need for pupils to be 'good' artists.

> *The way the department is, and the way it has become, has grown out of a principle of stripping away elite skills and allowing the pupils to enjoy the process of making art and see the value of learning through it.*
> Head of department, CAP identified school

This perspective on the inclusion of contemporary art seems to contradict the more popular conception that the teaching of skills is paramount, and that artistic references used to support the curriculum should be selected with this in mind. As discussed in Chapter 3, reactions to a series of images shown to interviewees suggested a desire to use artistic references conducive to the teaching of skills. This alternative view may suggest another form of achievement, associated more with the realisation of ideas than with the acquisition of skills.

4.3.2 The additional learning effects and outcomes of programmes including contemporary art practice

In the sample of schools in this research, where contemporary art practice was included in the curriculum it was always in addition to, rather than as a displacement of, more 'typical' approaches to art teaching. As indicated in section 4.2, the perceptions of the effects of the art curriculum were similar for teachers both in CAP and randomly identified schools. This section explores perceptions of how the inclusion of contemporary art practice produces different or enhanced outcomes and effects for pupils. Interviewees in CAP identified schools cited quite specific contributions to five of the seven categories of effects set out in section 4.2. Table 4.3 indicates the number of interviewees in the CAP identified schools citing impacts of contemporary art practice relating to each of those five effects.

Claims were made for the specific ways in which contemporary art practice contributed to each of the effects.

Table 4.3 The perceived learning effects and outcomes of programmes including contemporary art practice

Learning effects and outcomes	Percentage of teachers citing impact (number)
Art form knowledge and skills	33 (8)
Intrinsic and immediate effects	29 (7)
Creativity and thinking skills	16 (4)
Knowledge in the social and cultural domain	13 (3)
Communication and Expressive skills	13 (3)

N = 24 interviewees.
Most teachers indicated more than one impact, thus the categories are not mutually exclusive and percentages can sum up to more than 100 per cent.
Source: NFER interviews conducted with art teachers and heads of art departments in CAP identified schools (2003/2004)

Art form knowledge and skills: a wider understanding of what is art/what art can be

The most frequently cited outcome derived from the incorporation of contemporary art practice related to pupils' increased awareness and understanding of art. This outcome was cited by a third (33 per cent) of the interviewees in the CAP identified schools. As well as contributing more knowledge (of contemporary genres and current artists), contemporary art was seen as challenging existing knowledge. This included the way in which the inclusion of contemporary art practice increased pupils' awareness of art forms and the media and materials that can be used to produce art. It also included the way in which contemporary art could challenge pupils' perceptions of art as simply aesthetically pleasing, leading to a more developed understanding of art as a communication tool.

> *I think a lot of the stigmas attached to art are erased and it makes them really question what art is.*
> Art teacher, CAP identified school

As discussed in section 4.3.1, nine teachers cited this increased understanding of art as a reason for the inclusion of contemporary art practice.

Intrinsic and immediate effects: enhanced engagement with art as relevant to pupils' lives

The second most commonly perceived outcome related to the pupils' increased awareness of the ways in which art was relevant to their own lives (cited by approximately a third, 29 per cent, of the interviewees in the CAP identified schools). Whilst the study of art in general was seen to result in effects relating to enjoyment and fulfilment, it was thought that the study of contemporary art works to which pupils could relate specifically impacted on pupils' engagement with the subject and, thus, their enthusiasm for creating art.

> *I think they see a relationship to what is going on in real life. They don't feel they are looking at dead white European males. They can engage in their own practice as a practitioner and they can produce work that they want to produce.*
> Art teacher, CAP identified school

The perception that contemporary art is relevant to pupils' own lives and should therefore form part of the art curriculum delivered was cited as a reason for the inclusion of contemporary art practice by a total of 12 teachers (see section 4.3.1).

Creativity and thinking skills: the development of pupils' lateral thinking skills

The third most frequently cited outcome, cited by four (16 per cent) of the interviewees in the CAP identified schools, related to the development of pupils' creativity and thinking skills. It was claimed that studying contemporary art practice made a particular contribution to the development of pupils' lateral thinking skills. This was seen to result from the apparent freedom contemporary art provided for pupils to experiment with materials and ideas, think 'outside the box' and generally work in a more imaginative way. This was seen by a number of respondents to be in direct contrast to the perceived 'spoon-feeding' prevalent in other curriculum areas.

> *In other curriculum areas they are instructed as opposed to finding out for themselves. In art they have the opportunity to say 'I'm not sure how to do this but I am prepared to have a go and find out' – that's what education should be about.*
> Head of department, CAP identified school

Knowledge in the social and cultural domain: increased understanding of social, environmental and citizenship issues

Three teachers (13 per cent) referred to pupils' increased understanding of social, environmental and citizenship issues as a specific outcome of contemporary art practice. A higher proportion (33 per cent) of interviewees from this cohort cited this as an effect of the study of art in general. The exploration of such issues was primarily achieved through discussion of the themes presented in contemporary art and through the use of issues as stimuli for projects.

> *Looking at more conceptual artists inevitably means they have to think more about issues.*
>
> Head of department, CAP identified school

There is perhaps an implication here that the study of contemporary art may provide greater opportunities to address the National Curriculum aspiration: 'The study of art and design can contribute to an understanding of spiritual, ethical, social and citizenship issues' (QCA, 2003c, p.1).

Communication and expressive skills: increased visual communication skills

Lastly, three teachers (13 per cent) suggested that the inclusion of contemporary art practice contributed particularly to communication and expressive skills. Assertions were made concerning pupils' increased ability to view art as a medium for visual communication. Responses also focused on pupils' increased ability to express meaning and personal opinions through their work.

> *They get to learn lots of different ways of being able to communicate an idea. They learn how art work can be personal to them and they think about what they are trying to say in their art, whether it's a political or social statement or just about colour and shape.*
>
> Art teacher, CAP identified school

4.4 Summary and conclusions

Teachers in the full sample of schools identified a range of effects associated with the study of art in general that largely reflected the typology of effects proposed in Harland *et al*. (2000).

- The most commonly cited category of effects was art form knowledge and skills. This included the development of skills and techniques as well as increased awareness of artists and genres and art appreciation.

- Other categories of effects frequently referred to included knowledge in the social and cultural domain, personal and social development, and extrinsic transfer effects.

- The overall perceptions of the teachers in both cohorts of schools were similar and, for the most part, the limited amount of data collected through pupil interviewees supported the teachers' perspectives.

Teachers in the CAP identified schools were asked why they chose to incorporate contemporary art practice in their curriculum. The main reasons given for the inclusion of contemporary art were:

- to provide a curriculum that is more interesting, relevant and accessible to the pupils
- to increase pupils' understanding of the wider art world and challenge the notion of 'what is art?'
- to allow individual teacher preference for contemporary genres to be reflected in the curriculum taught.

None of the schools in the CAP identified sample displaced the more 'typical' overall curriculum design, based in a skills-led progression, with contemporary art practice. Instead, they enhanced and broadened their curriculum content, apparently with the intention of making it more inclusive in terms of pupil interest, teacher interest and the breadth of art studied. They did not seek to displace a skills-oriented approach, but rather to support it through the inclusion of contemporary art practice. However, they also appeared to be incorporating a greater attention to the exploration of meaning in art, and indeed to the meaning of art.

Interviewees suggested that the inclusion of contemporary art practice enhanced the more general effects of art education in the following ways:

- art form knowledge and skills, particularly a wider understanding of what is art/what art can be, through the study of contemporary art works
- intrinsic and immediate effects, focusing on the heightened awareness of the relevance of art to pupils' own lives and the subsequent effect this has on their motivation and enthusiasm for studying and creating art work
- creativity and thinking skills, particularly the development of pupils' lateral thinking skills
- knowledge in the social and cultural domain, primarily the increased understanding of social, environmental and citizenship issues through the study of issue-based art images
- communication and expressive skills, primarily increased visual communication skills, through the study of art for meaning.

This research does not suggest that these outcomes are not produced through curricula that do not include contemporary art practice, only that these are the particular claims made by those espousing contemporary art practice.

Questions for policy makers and practitioners

This final section poses some questions concerning the perceived impacts of art education and in particular the inclusion of contemporary art practice within school art. The questions have been framed in response to the findings discussed in this chapter.

- Is there an overemphasis placed on the acquisition of art form skills and knowledge (primarily art making skills and awareness of artists and genres) at the expense of creativity, lateral thinking, communication and expressive skills?

- Are teachers underestimating the importance of research skills as an outcome of art lessons and therefore neglecting to address it as a specific learning objective?

- Does a greater volume and range of art references necessarily generate greater art form knowledge?

- To what extent do teachers' own understanding of contemporary art impact on its inclusion in the curriculum? What are the implications of this for policy makers and gallery educators who are keen to encourage the inclusion of contemporary art practice?

- Is more research needed to investigate the claims made concerning the impact of contemporary art practice?

- Do the justifications for including contemporary art practice coincide with the views of policy makers and gallery educators who could enable the greater availability of contemporary art practice to schools?

- If the perceived impacts of contemporary art practice are confirmed would more initial and in-service teacher training be needed, in order to promote contemporary art practice to more teachers?

5 Implications for policy and practice in visual art teaching

5.1 Introduction

Having explored both the contents of the school art curriculum and the extent and nature of the inclusion of contemporary art practice in it in previous chapters, we now seek to look to the future.

This chapter raises a series of questions about the art curriculum as a whole, concerning the choice of curriculum content and, perhaps more fundamentally, issues around the purpose of art teaching. Included in this is whether contemporary art practice should be a more prominent feature of school art and, if so, how any such development could be achieved. It is not our intention to suggest an either/or resolution to any of the questions posed below, or to provoke positive or negative conclusions concerning contemporary art practice. Instead, we seek to set out some of the questions that seem to be already exercising teachers in the hope of stimulating further debate.

A summary of the context in which art teachers make their decisions concerning curriculum content, based on the discourse of interviewees in the sample is presented in section 5.2.

Section 5.3 poses some questions concerning the content of the curriculum in general and about the inclusion of contemporary art practice, both in terms of its manageability and its desirability.

Section 5.4 relates this study to previous research.

The chapter ends with a discussion of strategies that might be considered for further addressing the future development of the art curriculum (section 5.5).

5.2 The context within which art curriculum choices are made

All choices concerning the content of a curriculum have to take account of the context within which they are made. While there might be a variety of ambitions for what can be achieved in art education in schools, it may be that not all can be realised. Schools as institutions are unlike art colleges or the professional art world, serving different purposes and constrained by different considerations. Like the wider art world, they have long been an arena for conflicting philosophies and beliefs.

The most fundamental shared starting point for all art teaching in secondary schools is that it occurs in the context of a curriculum. All teachers in the sample were able to describe the overall structure of the curriculum within which their work took place. While the content may vary considerably, both in the planning and execution, all school art departments adopted a structure within which to teach a body of knowledge, skills and understanding in the realm of art. The concept of operating without a curriculum that identifies its structure and contents is generally inimical to a system of education. To venture into a course of study in which the contents are unknown is, in a sense, the antithesis of curriculum. In this fundamental sense, school art is inevitably different from the world of contemporary art production, in which forays into the unknown are a primary ambition. There was some indication of an assumption that pupils cannot 'go off at a tangent'. Whatever freedom teachers have to define the contents of a curriculum, the adoption of a curriculum, with inherent restriction, is assumed to be necessary.

It may also be argued that the education system makes an assumption that progression, achievement and, in many cases, qualifications stem from the curriculum. This must inevitably involve a process of assessment, with defined criteria, however flexible they may be and whoever takes on the role of assessing. It could be argued that the need to address assessment criteria in itself restricts, or at least partly directs, what is taught.

Neither the curriculum itself nor the process of assessment was seen by most teachers to be a restriction on the choice of content of art teaching in schools. But this does not necessarily mean that they were not restrictive. Once curriculum is defined, the assumption must be that it will be followed. One might argue therefore that if teachers do not report the curriculum as restrictive, they in fact mean that they agree with its contents – contents that they to a large extent have determined.

Interviewees were much more likely to report other contextual factors as restrictive. Limitations of time, both in amount and in arrangement (of short blocks, for example) and of funding for material resources were cited by many teachers, but by no means all. Whether the availability of time and resources, or teachers' attitudes to their availability, caused variation in their citation of restriction is unclear – some teachers may have less actual time and resources at their disposal, others may feel more restricted by availability. Whatever the cause of any difference in attitude to these factors, all art is taught in the context of finite space, time and resources. Therefore, choices need to be made concerning what to exclude from the curriculum, as well as what to include.

Teacher knowledge and expertise may also be seen as another resource affecting curriculum content. Teachers' knowledge of the range of artists and art images, and their expertise in particular art genres or media may well restrict curriculum content choices. Some teachers did acknowledge limitations in their breadth of knowledge of art movements and art history, with lack of familiarity with contemporary art practice being a particular area of weakness for some.

At various points in the interview process, several teachers alluded to pupil-related issues as factors that might affect curriculum content. Amongst these were pupil background and lack of familiarity with visual arts, and their potential negative responses to particular art images or concepts. It would appear that an upward pressure from pupils may have a considerable influence on the school art curriculum. Evidence from previous research (Harland *et al.*, 2000) indicates that pupils choose art as an option at GCSE partly as relief from an otherwise cerebral curriculum, seeking the satisfaction of doing or producing in art. Such an impulse may result in a form of collusion in which teachers choose to limit intellectual demands on pupils. Were this the case, the problem would be as much with the rest of the school curriculum as with art – if pupils need to retreat from the other subjects, perhaps those subjects need to generate a better balance between doing and thinking.

Any choices concerning the content of the curriculum will therefore have to be made in the context of the restrictions and limitations outlined. The data collected suggests that there are significant variations between schools and teachers in the content, scope and purposes of art teaching. In general terms, some schools appeared to offer a wider range and volume of art references in their teaching and there were also variations in the extent to which the curriculum focused on a skill-based approach rather than addressing meaning and issues through and in art. This research offered few indications that differences in school context accounted for differences in the choice of content or approach to art teaching.

Notwithstanding these limitations, there appeared to be considerable consensus that art teachers had substantial control over what is taught as school art. It is then difficult to avoid the conclusion that the scope to broaden the domain of school art rests firmly with art teachers and heads of department. The evidence presented in this research suggests substantial latitude on the part of teachers for growth and change. It therefore seems pertinent (if perhaps impertinent) to pose a series of questions to the profession and to policy makers about the nature and direction of potential transformative strategies.

This research does not assume that one approach to art teaching has greater validity than another – data was not gathered to correlate curriculum content with pupil achievement. Instead, the following section sets out a number of questions that spring from the findings reported in previous chapters. Most, but not all, relate to the potential contribution that the inclusion of contemporary art practice might make to the school art curriculum.

5.3 Questions raised from the research process

The following questions have been framed in response to the findings from the research process. It is assumed that most, if not all of them, are questions that already exercise the minds of those concerned with art teaching in secondary schools.

It is not our intention to suggest that there are two bodies of teachers that have opposing views on each of the questions posed below, rather that the findings from this research revealed no overall consensus on each of the questions identified.

Is a wider range of artistic genres or cultural references necessary for a more effective art education?

Before considering questions concerning the potential inclusion of contemporary art practice in the school art curriculum, some more fundamental issues need to be addressed. In commissioning the research, the sponsors had suggested that there may be a 'prevailing orthodoxy' in school art teaching, characterised in part by the limited range of art genres and art references being addressed by teachers. Chapter 2 suggested that there is evidence from some schools to support that view. However, the research offers no evidence to suggest that there is anything inherently unsatisfactory about any such limitation. As indicated in section 5.2, there is an inevitable limit to what can be fitted into the curriculum and to the breadth of artistic knowledge of any individual art teacher, or indeed of any art department collectively. Does that of itself render the teaching of art less effective or less appropriate? Some teachers in CAP identified schools claimed that a wider range of references were necessary for enhancing pupils' understanding of art. However, it is arguable that a narrower range of references enables teachers to teach more effectively, playing to a greater depth rather than breadth of knowledge or expertise. It is possible that the introduction of too many genres or artistic references could be confusing and dissipating. However, it may also be the case that the wider the range of options available to teachers, the more likely they are to be able to select genres and images that are appropriate to their particular purposes, and indeed their particular pupils. It might also be argued that key stage 3 amounts, in some respects, to a taster course, and should therefore give pupils the widest possible artistic 'menu' so that they can identify what interests them. This might be seen as a compelling argument given that key stage 4 is so widely seen as the stage at which pupils can make their own decisions concerning those aspects of art that they choose to explore in greater depth.

Does the apparent concentration on painting and drawing exclude other media such as sculpture, design and photography, and what are the educational repercussions of this?

While it is appreciated that various resource and logistical issues militate against the use of other media, particularly 3D media, it is also the case that some contemporary art practice ventures into the use of new media, opening opportunities for new forms of expression. For example, ICT as a medium for art creation has become much more accessible to young people in their everyday lives, but this has not, apparently, been substantially reflected in the content of school art. It may be that a gap is growing between young people's experience of artistic production and consumption in their home and social lives and that which they experience in school art. It may well be argued that it is not the place of the school curriculum to replicate other experiences of young people, rather to extend them and offer alternatives. It might also be argued that exploiting young people's existing interests and experiences can provide a starting point for challenging and extending learning.

Are critical analysis, issue-based learning and the communication of meaning in and through art sufficiently integrated and balanced with the acquisition of the craft skills of art making?

The teaching of art skills was regarded by the large majority of interviewees as the bedrock of the curriculum, especially in key stage 3. Consideration of issues or the expression and understanding of meaning in art attracted much less attention from interviewees, and it was largely undertaken at key stage 4. As suggested earlier, there may be some pressure from pupils to maintain an art curriculum that concentrates more on making art than on thinking about art. However, there are those who suggest that art provides a route through which young people can explore issues that are pertinent to them, and that they welcome the opportunity to do so. Some pupils may well find a visual, rather than a linguistic route into intellectual exercise more manageable and appealing. Some interviewees in the sample were at pains to point out that they were not creating the next generation of artists, but were instead seeking to educate pupils through the study of art. Given that art is part of the cultural heritage of any country, it might also be argued that an intellectual exploration of the context and content of art would therefore provide a valuable contribution to cultural (and intercultural) understanding. This research offers no evidence that paying more attention to issues and meaning had the effect of deterring pupils from opting for art. It may be appropriate to reconsider the balance between developing art skills, accompanied by the apparently therapeutic value of doing so, and the distinct opportunities for intellectual challenge afforded by the study of art. Some interviewees suggested that the inclusion of contemporary art practice in the curriculum stimulated in pupils an appetite for intellectual engagement that other art genres did not.

Is the limited creative use of ICT in art, as opposed to its use for art research, a shortcoming given the emphasis placed on the use of ICT within the curriculum as whole?

ICT has been promoted throughout the school curriculum over recent years, to the extent that all subjects are expected to demonstrate their contribution to pupils' learning in that area. While the description of modules suggests that considerable use is made of ICT as a medium for research, especially through the internet, there was only limited evidence of ICT being used as a medium for creating art by pupils. This may be driven by a lack of available technology or of teacher expertise in using ICT as an art making medium. It may even be a deliberate policy on the part of some teachers wishing to ensure that pupils learn the direct physical skills of art making before using an electronic alternative. Exploration of ICT by contemporary artists has led to entirely new forms of artistic representation that do not ape work produced in more conventional art media. This, and the interest and expertise in ICT being developed by pupils in their own time and using their own resources, may be an opportunity waiting to be grasped in more schools.

Is sufficient attention being paid in art to the teaching of research skills and, in particular, the critical use of the internet?

The data gathered during this research suggested that, while pupils are required to undertake a considerable amount of research in art, perhaps they are not being taught the skills needed to do so effectively. Teachers have expressed frustration that pupils simply download information from the internet without any critical judgement or even any attempt to understand it. Few teachers referred to research as a skill that they taught in their modules, but did refer to it as an activity undertaken by pupils, often in their own time, in support of modules. In the limited number of pupil interviews there was frequent reference to research as a skill that could be transferred to other learning areas. Teachers were much less likely to cite such an outcome. It may well be that the visual appeal of art images on the internet could provide pupil motivation and a considerable opportunity for the teaching of research skills. Again, access to computers may inhibit this activity in some cases.

While seeking to reveal in more detail the overall content of the art curriculum as delivered in schools, this research paid particular attention to the place of contemporary art practice in school art. In doing so, a range of often conflicting views emerged concerning both the manageability and the desirability of broadening the curriculum generally. Some of these differences appeared to be polarised and some more graduated. These differences are addressed through the following questions.

Is contemporary art practice an appropriate component of the school art curriculum?

A wide spectrum of views on this issue emerged from the research. At one end there were those who believed that contemporary art practice, and in particular more conceptual art, were not suitable for study during key stages 3 and 4 and should wait until after the compulsory school years, either at art college or at least until key stage 5. There were others who believed that it should be added to, rather than replace, the more conventional practices studied through art teaching in key stages 3 and 4. Although none argued for entirely displacing a more traditional and conventionally skill-based art curriculum with contemporary art practice, evidence in one school suggested that their approach was largely guided by principles associated with contemporary art practice.

Both logistical and philosophical reasons were cited for taking positions on this issue and the following questions are ordered as a progression from the apparently more logistical issues, through to more philosophical ones.

Can contemporary art practice be accessed effectively for inclusion in the school art curriculum?

It would appear that some teachers are more conversant with contemporary art practice than others. This may well be in part due to their own interest and motivation, but may also be partly accounted for by practical issues such as access to contemporary art exhibitions, awareness of sources of information and the potential to be involved in CPD opportunities addressing contemporary art practice. Each of these was cited by teachers in the research as possible reasons for not including contemporary art practice. Another possible obstacle to the inclusion of contemporary art practice amongst artistic and cultural references was deemed to be the difficulty of physically presenting some contemporary art work to pupils. It was seen as inadequate to use 2D representations of some 3D art pieces, and installation or time-based works could not be brought into schools. While some schools had realistic access to galleries or venues showing such work, others did not.

There were also seen to be obstacles to introducing art making activities involving contemporary art practice. For example, it may not be possible for some schools to accommodate 3D work requiring considerable space, or expensive and unusual materials. The shortage of dedicated computers was seen, albeit rarely, as an obstacle to developing digital art work, though whether lack of equipment resulted in lack of appetite for such work, or vice versa, was unclear.

Would the inclusion of contemporary art practice support the fuller achievement of the aims of the National Curriculum for art (as defined in QCA documents)?

The view was expressed that contemporary art practice tended to be too obscure or intellectually challenging for many pupils to grasp, and that to include it might have the effect of alienating pupils, thus reducing their chance of achievement in or through art. However, the apparently greater focus on spiritual, moral and social issues in those schools that did incorporate contemporary art practice might suggest that contemporary art practice is a valuable resource in delivering that aspect of the curriculum. Much depends here on the extent to which the curriculum is seen to be fundamentally about the acquisition of skills to the detriment of the exploration of meaning or understanding. QCA guidelines indicate that both need to be addressed – it would appear that schools have the responsibility of setting the balance between them. This research does not assume that a curriculum without contemporary art practice cannot deliver both, merely that those espousing contemporary art practice claim it to be a particularly effective tool for doing this.

Is contemporary art practice intellectually, emotionally and socially accessible to students in school?

Of all of the questions posed here, this one elicited perhaps the most polarised views amongst teachers. When asked to respond to certain images, it became clear that some were resisted by teachers on the grounds that pupils would not understand them. This was occasionally accompanied by an admission that the teacher did not understand them either. Even concerning the same image, one teacher could regard it as incomprehensible to pupils while another regarded it as entirely accessible. There is no evidence to suggest that this difference in assertions was based on varying pupil capacity to understand. Responses to the set of images also suggested that some teachers believed that their pupils would react adversely to some contemporary art by becoming bored, disruptive or offended. It was suggested that some images might be too close to the experience of pupils and therefore cause offence. Others felt that because it was so close to their experience, they would be more likely to engage with it. This might suggest a preference on the part of some teachers to remain in a 'comfort zone' of familiarity and manageability of pupil responses and to avoid exposure to or discussion of issues that might involve problematic responses. It is possible, but not apparent in the research, that differences in social backgrounds between schools could account for these different standpoints. Alternatively, the personal attitude of the teacher may be responsible. Another reason may well be divergent views on the purpose of addressing art – that some teachers are more active than others in seeking to challenge and disturb pupils' perceptions either of art or of their social environment. Do their view differs from those resisting contemporary art practice in that they see more potential in works of contemporary art, or do they have a larger range of contemporary references at their disposal, from which they can choose the most appropriate images? This is not immediately apparent from the data. However, the fact that they are likely to incorporate a much greater volume and range of artistic references in their teaching, from a wider range of artistic genres and periods, suggests that the latter may well be the case.

Are teachers equipped with the knowledge and understanding to incorporate contemporary art practice in their teaching?

A small minority of teachers expressed the view that they were not. Others were clearly confident about their own engagement with contemporary art, for reasons that are explored in Chapter 3. The relationship between motivation and expertise is complex and it may well be that a combination of lack of knowledge of, or enthusiasm for, contemporary art accounts for its lesser use by some teachers. Teachers themselves perceive a lack of significant CPD opportunities relating to ICT or current developments in the wider art world. This may be related to location, lack of funding or lack of time to avail themselves of those opportunities that did exist. Several indicated that they would appreciate more support in acquiring the necessary information, knowledge and understanding of contemporary art practice. There was evidence of an appetite for CPD that was directly related to art itself, rather than to art teaching. Teachers in CAP identified schools were more likely to be, or have been, practising artists in their own right. It may well be worth exploring whether the Artist Teacher Scheme, which enables teachers to develop their capacity as artists, also results in a broader or more eclectic art curriculum, both in its content and purposes. (The Artist Teacher Scheme is an expanding creative professional development programme for teachers and lecturers in art and design.)

Is the freedom of choice of teachers to define art curriculum content an appropriate method of selecting the cultural and artistic references to be included?

It would appear that art teachers, either as individuals or as school-level collectives, have very considerable control over what they include in their curriculum content. It may be a compelling suggestion that art teaching is well-served by teachers working in areas for which they have particular enthusiasm and expertise. Such a freedom may or may not be more appropriate in the case of art teaching than in other subjects. However, it may be worth considering the extent to which that choice is based on personal (or departmental) predilection, on pupil need, comfort or interest, or on the specific aims of the curriculum as defined in schools. Although this may be a provocative suggestion, it may be appropriate to explore further how decisions concerning curriculum content are made in schools and whether, in the interest of improving curriculum entitlement for all pupils, the National Curriculum should specify a broader range of cultural references and artistic media.

Whether or not these questions have already been addressed by the profession, there is clearly no broad consensus concerning answers to them. This may well be regarded as a strength of art education, in that it indicates an inclusive and liberal approach to the subject. However, the questions remain and could provide a frame within which productive discourse might lead to further understanding.

5.4 Contribution to the body of research into visual art learning in schools

The literature review indicated the existence of a considerable amount of research concerning the place of the arts in school, and there is also a wealth of papers advocating the role that the arts, including visual art, can play in the overall education of young people. There are also studies of specific arts projects, often involving partnerships between artists and educators, most of which are short term and relating to a very specific aspect of the art form.

This research builds on the findings of those studies that have explored the art curriculum in schools. Previous assertions concerning the tendency of the curriculum to focus more on skills than on meaning have been supported by the findings of this research. The effects of art education documented elsewhere have also been corroborated through the perceptions of interviewees.

This research offers additional evidence concerning the tendency of teachers to use a limited number of art references in supporting their teaching, and pays particular attention to the factors, both contextual and personal, that may determine their selection of what to include in the curriculum. By focusing on descriptions of the content of modules it has been possible to indicate more specifically the nature of any 'bias'. It has also provided more evidence concerning the bases upon which curriculum content choices are made. By bringing together purely descriptive accounts of curriculum content with teachers' perceptions of issues affecting their choices, as well as their immediate reactions to a sample of art images, it has been possible to build up a picture of what decisions are made, backed by some understanding of why they are made.

Although only working from a fairly small sample, it has been possible to make some indication of the quantities of references and the breadth of curriculum approaches. It has also been possible to identify characteristics that are shared by schools that are known to address contemporary art practice as part of their curriculum. However, it should be stressed that the more significant common denominators for such schools may well be that they draw on a wider range of art references (contemporary or otherwise) and espouse a more inclusive view of the purposes of art learning. It may well be that embracing contemporary art practice is simply a manifestation of these more inclusive approaches to art teaching.

5.5 Possible future strategies to address issues concerning art curriculum content

The findings from this research do not suggest that the art curriculum overall is either enhanced or impeded by the inclusion of contemporary art practice. It was not the remit of the research to correlate outcomes (for example, in the form of examination results, pupil achievement or a range of other actual effects) with the content of the curriculum as delivered in different schools. There is no assumption of 'right answers' to any of the questions posed in section 5.3.

One of the most striking findings from this research is the extent to which individual teachers not only determine how they teach art, but also what they include as curriculum content. It also emerged that they were attached in varying degrees to a variety of aims for an art education at secondary school level. The capacity to tailor the aims and content of the curriculum to suit local, and indeed individual, needs and interests may be seen not only as a great strength, but also as a great opportunity. If, as this research suggests, there are such variations in curriculum approach, there is also the opportunity for development of a dialectic that might further promote the consideration and refinement of the curriculum.

Curriculum development is sometimes seen as the responsibility of policy makers, either at academic or governmental level. In the case of art, that responsibility seems to rest, to a considerable degree, with teachers. Those that have an interest in promoting the place of contemporary art practice in schools will therefore need to address the needs and interests of that constituency as well as engaging with education policy makers. Although not an area for investigation in this research, it has become apparent that considerable efforts are already being made both to encourage and enable art teachers to embrace contemporary art practice in their teaching. Several interviewees referred to the value of such efforts, but also to the scarcity of opportunities. There were also calls for more support in this field, for example in the form of information concerning exhibitions, courses, publications and websites. For example, it was asserted that schools needed considerably more advance notice of exhibitions if they were to plan visits into the school calendar. Doubtless, much information of this kind is already in the public domain, and in many cases is already targeted at teachers.

Such support, in the form of inputs, may be very helpful. However, there may be greater potential in stimulating and enabling a dialogue concerning the curriculum, firstly between art teachers themselves, and secondly between art teachers and the contemporary art community. While some teachers may need, and value, greater information and understanding about the educational potential of contemporary art practice, that cannot be provided unless the aspirations and preoccupations of art teachers are more fully understood by those offering information and support.

It is hoped that this research reveals some of the considerations affecting the ways in which teachers relate to the role of contemporary art practice in schools. Encouraging a dialogue with them on these issues, hearing their concerns, understanding the constraints affecting their teaching and, above all, hearing their views on the purpose of art teaching should be priorities for those wishing to promote contemporary art practice in schools.

While particularly focused on contemporary art practice (or its absence) in schools, this research has also provided some evidence to support the assertion that the range of art genres and references in school art in general is limited. It might also be argued that those schools that had been identified as already engaged with contemporary art practice had a generally more eclectic approach in their art teaching than the randomly identified schools. The real distinction may be that some schools offer a wider range of references, of which contemporary art practice is only one. Such schools also appeared to embrace a wider or more balanced approach to aims in their art teaching. It may be appropriate for any debate and dialogue to focus more on these distinctions than specifically on the issues of contemporary art practice. The absence of any succinct definition of contemporary art practice, and the apparent preference of some teachers to avoid or eschew any such categorisation, might suggest that this broader debate could produce more fertile discussion. Why we include art in the curriculum, and what sort of content could best support our purposes, remain the real questions. In a changing world those questions may need constant attention.

Appendix 1 Research into visual art learning: a literature review

A1 Introduction

This chapter presents the findings of the research into visual art learning literature review and accompanies the NFER report on research into visual art learning at key stage 3 and 4. The review has been updated to include new or newly identified literature throughout the course of the project from August 2003 to August 2004.

A2 Methodology

The NFER Library conducted searches for existing literature concerning the content of the secondary art curriculum in accordance with the proposal.

> *The study would start with a review of the relevant existing literature on research carried out in England since the introduction of the National Curriculum in 1989. Essentially, the review would focus on studies of the content of the school art curriculum as implemented, especially that provided at key stages 3 and 4. It would also explore whether any 'grey' unpublished information could be made available through agencies such as the (Qualification and Curriculum Authority) QCA. The report of the review would document the main findings presented in the literature.*

Key and relevant databases were identified by researchers and by the library. Full details of the searches can be found in the search strategy (see page 141).

The initial search of UK databases produced approximately 50 citings, and was extended to include European and English speaking overseas. The combined searches provided approximately 500 citings, from which those most relevant to the research were selected.

For the most part, items have been excluded that appear to be advocacy or position papers, with the exception of those that may inform the researchers' preparation for the future phase of this research. QCA documents, Ofsted guidelines and other assorted publications have also been included, where it was felt they would provide useful context for the review and the research project as a whole.

Each document received was read and summarised, and categorised using the following sub-headings:

- research based, focusing on content and foci of visual art curriculum in secondary schools, UK based (only one document was identified as being based on empirical research, concerned with secondary art education and focusing particularly on the content of the UK curriculum)
- research based, UK based, arts in general (a total of eight identified)
- case study, action research, self study (a total of eight identified)
- discussion papers (a total of 18 identified)
- other (a total of eight identified).

A3 Editorial summary

The literature searches conducted by NFER library found only a limited selection of research concerned specifically with the curriculum content of secondary school art. A substantial amount of research considers the place of the arts as a whole within the school curriculum. Whilst this reveals a positive attitude amongst teachers to the teaching of the arts, including visual arts, there is little consideration of the form that this teaching takes or the content of the curriculum delivered. Research is currently underway in the United States to ascertain how the visual arts are taught. The two year project by the University of Harvard's educational research group, Project Zero, aims to analyse teaching in the visual arts and identify the concepts and techniques employed by art educators in the United States. No current UK research of this nature was discovered.

Those documents reviewed that did address the content of the art curriculum, for the most part look at particular aspects, for example, the use of ICT or the pedagogy for developing critical theory, rather than curriculum content as a whole. However, they reveal relevant issues about the teaching of art, which may have implications for the content of the curriculum and the inclusion of contemporary practices.

To maximise the benefits of the literature review, the following section has been structured to cover the research questions to be addressed in the main research phase. Three key questions were posed for the literature review.

- What is 'school art' at key stage 3 and 4?

- What are its main foci and contents?
- In what ways are pupils encouraged to broaden their approaches to the process of engaging with art forms and genres?

These are initially explored simultaneously. They are then explored individually in more depth in the concluding summary.

A3.1 Curriculum content of the art curriculum

- What is 'school art' at key stage 3 and 4?
- What are its main foci and contents?
- In what ways are pupils encouraged to broaden their approaches to the process of engaging with art forms and genres?

There is very little empirical evidence in the reviewed literature to suggest the overall content of the art curriculum at key stages 3 and 4. However, to provide a context to the review, the QCA programme of study for key stage 3 and other relevant documentation have been included. The overall aim of the National Curriculum key stage 3 programme of study for art and design is that:

> *Teaching should ensure that investigating and making includes exploring and developing ideas and evaluating and developing work. Knowledge and understanding should inform this process.*
> QCA (2003c)

Whilst QCA provides schemes of work that include specific artists, topics and skills and prescribes that a range of artists and genres must be studied, the actual curriculum content employed to achieve these objectives is at the individual teacher's discretion. Key stage 4 art and design curricula are defined by the schools' chosen examining boards' programmes of study. As with the QCA documentation, these tend to be objective-based rather than content and foci specific.

The empirical research studies included in this review concentrate on the arts as a whole within education, as opposed to specific curriculum foci. Ross and Kamba (1997) and Harland *et al.* (2000) are two such studies. In both studies the general attitude of educational practitioners emerged as supportive of the arts. Congruently the pupils involved in both projects agreed that the arts were an important part of their education.

The findings within Ross and Kamba (1997) were extensive, as the project considers all art forms. Art and design emerged as the most popular arts subject from the pupil's perspective. The study also sought to ascertain the possible objectives for teaching the arts. The priorities for teaching visual art conformed to that of the other art forms, with personal development and self-expression emerging as key objectives. Although this does not reveal any more about the nature of school art, it does provide some contextual data about why school art is taught.

Harland *et al.* (2000) also found that visual art was the 'strongest' of the art subjects. The data revealed that more students elected to study art for GCSE and the perceived benefits were greater, from the teacher's perspective, than they were for the other art forms. The focus of the research was on the effects of art teaching and are documented by typology of effect as opposed to art form. However, the effects of art teaching are given separately in the conclusion and, as with the priorities for teaching that emerged in Ross and Kamba (1997), art shares generic effects with the other art forms. Effects identified as being art specific emerged as the development of art knowledge and skills, extrinsic transfer effects, and intrinsic and immediate effects.

Research undertaken as part of the QCA's development project in the arts (Hargreaves and Lamont, 2002) also considers the attitudes of educational practitioners. As with the above study, this research found that teachers and school managers valued the arts and that the arts have maintained their place in the curriculum despite increasing time pressures and a lack of resources. Of the four art forms considered (art, drama, music and dance) art, or art and design, was highlighted as having the most available resources and overall it was allocated the most time within the curriculum structure. Despite this, there was a general consensus that time limitations were causing the arts to be taught through knowledge and skills-based approaches, with the distinct possibility that more conceptual approaches and notions of creativity were being neglected.

The changes in the teaching of art and design highlighted in Ross and Kamba (1997) and Hargreaves and Lamont (2002) may have implications for the inclusion of contemporary art practices, which are often seen as lending themselves to a more conceptual-based pedagogy, concerned with thinking skills as opposed to motor skills.

This view is shared by Hughes (1998), who states that pupils are limited in their opportunities to explore 'stylistic orthodoxies', which he goes on to describe as 'mirroring more closely the strategies adopted by contemporary professional practitioners' (p. 42).

Other, smaller scale studies concentrate more on what constitutes an effective curriculum than on the content of the current curriculum. Barrett (1990) carried out a series of observations of primary school children in their art lessons. Based on these observations she suggests the need for an art curriculum that provides opportunities for the development of skills, objective enquiry and expressive responses, and highlights the need for defining a purpose and value of art teaching when designing the curriculum. Although primary based, this paper concludes that a good art education at primary level can provide children with the critical awareness and evaluation skills needed for development at key stages 3 and 4.

In conclusion, existing research reveals much about the current position of the visual arts within the school curriculum, but is very limited in its descriptions of its content, the media in which pupils are working, or the ways in which they are encouraged to explore these media. Whilst art emerges as one of the most 'robust art forms' (Harland *et al.*, 2000), there still appears to be limited research into the way in which it is delivered. The extent to which contemporary art may form part of the content of school art, or the degree to which contemporary art thinking influences pedagogy is explored in the following sections. The three questions addressed in this section will be considered in more detail towards the end of the review, in order to draw some conclusions about the current content of the school art curriculum.

A3.2 The inclusion of contemporary art in the art curriculum

- To what extent is 'contemporary art practice' represented in the key stages 3 and 4 curriculum?
- How do teachers incorporate 'contemporary art practice' within the key stages 3 and 4 art curriculum and across the curriculum?

As discussed earlier, data within the literature defining the exact nature of the content being delivered at key stages 3 and 4 is limited. Therefore, it is difficult to draw conclusions from the literature concerning the extent to which contemporary art practice is represented. However, two action-based research projects included in the review offer an insight into ways in which the authors have incorporated contemporary art into their own practice.

Long (2001) describes an eight month project in which year 10 students worked with multimedia software for a proportion of their art lessons. The theme for the project was 'movement'. Students looked at the work of contemporary artists who were using multimedia forms to explore similar starting points. They also considered the work of artists in more traditional media, but who had also taken movement as their stimulus.

The students involved initially found it hard to share their teacher's perception that the moving images they were producing were legitimate 'art'. However, throughout the course of the project Long believes that the students began to broaden their horizons and by the end were able to 'appreciate the blurring boundaries between fine art and popular form' (Long, 2001, p.260). This widening of pupils' perceptions was also noted by Loveless (2003) in the evaluation of a project providing opportunities for students to work with professional digital artists and explore the use of ICT in their work.

Although deemed an overall success, Long felt that this approach to incorporating contemporary art practice in schools was not without its drawbacks. The major drawback, from the perspective of the teacher involved, was that much of the work had to be done in the ICT suite and not in the art room. This meant that the suite needed to be free during timetabled art lessons and increased file space on the school network was required.

> *Overcoming these problems typifies the situation for many teachers of art and design in UK schools. Computer facilities are likely to be organised around the Business Education/IT departments and the file space allocated to pupils reflects an expectation that outcomes from software like Word or Excel will be stored rather than imagery of any kind.*
> Long (2001, p.258)

Callow (2001) describes another stand-alone project, involving the use of digital photography in art lessons. Unlike the Long (2001) project, in this instance the art department had access to its own computer and the school as a whole had recently increased its ICT provision. This was seen as a key facilitating factor in the success of this project. In this study contemporary practice was brought into the curriculum in the form of a two-day workshop run by a professional local digital artist. With the assistance of the teacher the children created digital images based on the working title of 'Inner-Self'. The teacher, the artist and the students involved are documented as being happy with the work they produced and again it is felt that working in a new media such as this helped to expand the students' concept of what can be called 'art'.

The studies cited here offer ideas for the inclusion of contemporary art, and begin to suggest the possible value for students. However, the evaluations are based on stand-alone projects and whilst they begin to make suggestions, do not provide researched strategies for the long-term inclusion of contemporary art.

A3.3 Barriers to the inclusion of contemporary art in the art curriculum

- What are the barriers within the school context to the inclusion of contemporary art practice in the key stages 3 and 4 art curriculum?

As discussed earlier, some practitioners are finding ways of incorporating contemporary art practice into their lessons. However, the literature reviewed revealed a number of barriers within the school context to the inclusion of contemporary art. It is also feasible that a number of external, contextual factors may be limiting the amount of contemporary art taught in schools. These will be considered in more detail in section A4.

The issue of censorship as a possible barrier to the inclusion of contemporary art is raised by Emery (2002). This paper discusses research designed to ascertain teachers' reasons for including or censoring a particular artist or art works in their lessons. The study found that the teachers interviewed did not openly censor art works for inclusion and felt that contemporary images could provide a useful way of allowing students to explore more complex issues through art. However, the lack of available resources on controversial artists and the 'readiness' of the students to deal with the issues raised in more contentious art works were cited as possible reasons why contemporary art was deemed less appropriate for use in the classroom.

Burgess (2003) suggests that teachers are reluctant to include contemporary art in the curriculum because they consider it too difficult a subject area to approach. She cites Hutchinson (1998) who comments that contemporary art is often perceived as 'an art full of monsters, replete with vulgarity and coarseness…' In addition, Burgess argues that its inclusion also runs the risk of rebuke from senior managers and parents, suggesting that the culture of individual schools may be a potential barrier.

Callow (2001), Sinker (2001), Loveless (2003) and Rogers and Bacon (2002) all found that a lack of available resources, including materials and appropriately equipped arts spaces, presented a major barrier to the inclusion of contemporary art practice. Callow (2001) notes that, in order for the art curriculum to keep up to date with developments in the art world and visual culture, including digital imagery, ICT software needs to be an integral part of the art curriculum. In order for this to happen, art teachers and school managers need to be aware of the potential uses of ICT and art spaces need to be equipped accordingly. Although not based on empirical evidence, the author feels that this is not currently the case in the majority of secondary schools in the UK.

Sinker (2001) goes on to state that, even when resources are made available, existing curriculum restraints prevent teachers making full use of them. The study pulls together data collected from teachers involved in the piloting of the DARE website, a digital art resource for school use. The teachers involved stated that they were supportive of the resource. However, they found it difficult to find the time to research it in depth and therefore to adapt it for use in the classroom. This suggests an apparent lack of freedom, related to time pressures, which may prevent teachers from incorporating new and contemporary art into their lessons, even when new resources are available.

In an evaluation of an existing ICT in art project (Art on the Net), Loveless (2003) found that art teachers did not have the access to ICT equipment required in order for ICT to become a part of the art curriculum. In agreement with Callow (2001), this evaluation found that art rooms were not equipped accordingly and that most of the access to ICT equipment was through the use of ICT suites. These suites present their own problems in that they require booking in advance, are often in a different part of the school building from the art department and are not set up in such a way that easily facilitates the making and sharing of art work. Loveless (2003) suggests that the profile of the art department in the school needs to be raised when discussions about the placing of ICT resources are taking place. This way, the need for ICT equipment, including software, which is both relevant and available to the art department, can be considered, instead of a generic approach to the provision of equipment that is often adopted by schools. Teachers involved in this evaluation also commented that, even when resources were made available to them, as was the case in the Art on the Net project, they did not always have the skills or prior experience of using ICT for producing art. It was also felt that pupils themselves may struggle with the skills needed for using ICT in a creative way. Despite having extensive previous use of computers, this had tended to be centred around office-based skills, and not on the creative applications of image manipulation software. This has implications both for teacher in-service training (INSET) and the nature of the ICT curriculum as delivered to students, and would require a broader perspective on the use of ICT to be adopted.

Rogers and Bacon (2002) found changes in the curriculum away from the traditional 'working on A4 paper' to the inclusion of 3D and multimedia work, meant that the requirements of an art space were changing. Flexibility was required within art spaces to allow for new and innovative art work.

Three-quarters of secondary schools in a survey of teachers (Rogers *et al.*, 2004) stated that the quality of their art department accommodation meant they were unable to offer key disciplines – such as photography, 3D work and sculpture. Restrictive art spaces themselves may, therefore, be another barrier to the inclusion of more contemporary art forms being addressed in schools.

Whilst the benefits of its inclusion are recognised, the studies are consistent in their opinion that contemporary art, in the present educational system, is not as easily accessible or adaptable for classroom practice as more traditional genres. This is largely perceived to be a result of physical environments and lack of resources. It is worth noting at this point that the studies reviewed concentrate on contemporary art defined by the use of new or contemporary media, for example, ICT. To date, no research has been identified that considers contemporary practice as a process, when applied to more traditional media. Whilst the above studies do highlight the barriers to the inclusion of contemporary media they provide little evidence concerning the inclusion or exemption of contemporary art practice.

A3.4 External contextual factors affecting the inclusion of contemporary art

- What external contextual factors might be influencing the status of contemporary art in key stages 3 and 4?

By looking at the QCA documentation and other background resources included in this review it is possible to draw out some external contextual factors that may be influencing the status of contemporary art.

As discussed in section A1, the QCA programme of study for art and design: key stage 3 outlines the general requirements of the art curriculum. It stresses the importance of ensuring that students have opportunities to explore and develop ideas through investigating, making and evaluating their work. In order to achieve this overall aim the QCA documentation highlights the need for teachers to ensure pupils are taught knowledge, skills and understanding in a variety of ways. The breadth of study suggested includes 'using a range of materials and processes, including ICT' and 'investigating art in a variety of genres, styles and traditions' (QCA, 2003c).

This programme of study does not appear to have negative implications for the status of contemporary art. Moreover, it provides opportunities for the exploration of contemporary genres and innovative media. However, analysis of the suggested schemes of work to accompany this programme of study revealed very few examples of the inclusion of contemporary genres.

Unit 9b: 'Change your style' asks pupils to 'explore contemporary designs' as part of a process of understanding art and design in a wider cultural context. It includes work on evaluating art works by exploring the genre in which they are produced. Whilst it suggests the exploration of contemporary designs, it is in no way prescriptive and the unit can be successfully completed without including contemporary art (QCA, 2003b).

Unit 8b: 'Animating art' requires pupils to 'explore the use of moving image to communicate ideas'. This scheme of work provides scope for the inclusion of contemporary art media such as photography and digital imaging. It stresses the importance of including contemporary visual culture in the art curriculum, but as such is in a minority of units (QCA, 2003a).

The AQA GCSE art and design specification for examination in 2004 onwards is an indicator of the programmes of study set by UK examining boards. The overall aims, intended to set out the purpose of GCSE courses in art and design, include encouraging candidates to develop 'creative and imaginative powers, and the practical skills for communicating and expressing feelings and meanings in art, craft and design' (AQA, 2002, p.11). An art-based curriculum at key stage 4, therefore, may be seen as more inclusive of an investigative and communicative approach, in which contemporary art practices may have a role. This is in comparison to the key stage 3 curriculum, which, for the most part, is concerned with skills and knowledge as opposed to critical or conceptual thinking.

Inspectors working on behalf of Ofsted are advised to look for evidence that children are being encouraged to work in different media, both 2D and 3D, and are given opportunities to explore 'the work of a range of artists, craftspeople and designers, from different times and cultures' (Ofsted, 2001, p.9). Whilst this does not create a barrier to contemporary art, neither does it specifically encourage its inclusion.

A considerable number of the discussion papers included in the review make reference to the constraints of the National Curriculum and identify assessment objectives as the main contextual factors influencing the teaching of art. Binch (1994), Pringle (2002), Long (2001) and Hughes (1998) all cite rigid curriculum structures, prioritisation of the core subjects and general constraints on time for art teaching as key factors that may be limiting the freedom for innovative and contemporary work. Whilst 'art' in the professional art world is able to embrace new technologies and move itself forward as a radical and often challenging activity, school art appears restricted by the culture in which it operates.

> *The National Curriculum and the control imposed by external assessment and current methods of inspection are increasingly seen as an unnecessary constricting straight jacket, which militates creative pedagogy and bears little relation to concepts of art and design as they are exemplified in further and higher education and the world of the professional artist and designer.*
> Hughes (1999, p.130)

However, Hulks (2003) argues that this negative perception of the impact of assessment on the art curriculum is not necessarily justifiable. He suggests that an effective assessment regime, intelligently applied, can in fact encourage 'aesthetic sophistication'. Teachers' fears that creativity in art classrooms would inevitably be reduced by introducing assessment systems have proved unsubstantiated and Hulks argues that, in practice, the impact has been negligible.

Therefore the National Curriculum guidelines, in terms of prescribed content, are not in themselves an inhibitor.

This view is supported by Burgess (2003) who highlights the flexibility within the National Curriculum, in particular the way it was designed to be a framework in which teachers could develop their own ideas. She suggests that any restrictions on the art studied and the pedagogies employed at secondary level are not as a result of the curriculum itself but of the way in which it has been interpreted.

> *Unfortunately, too few secondary teachers have interpreted it as an opportunity to extend their practice, adopting instead a literal (mis)reading which merely validated existing orthodoxies.*
> Burgess (2003, p.109)

Burgess blames this resistance to move away from existing orthodoxies on the 'weight of heritage' that is holding back school art practice. She cites modern subjects such as sociology and media studies as subjects that do incorporate more contemporary approaches, and concludes that it is tradition, and a reluctance to move away from it, that prevents visual art from adopting a similar approach.

Binch (1994) agrees that the National Curriculum for art is relatively content free and that teachers have considerable choice in the kinds of experiences they provide for children. However, he argues that the National Curriculum and GCSEs are assessment-led. Curriculum development is controlled and limited by attainment targets and end of key stage statements. Despite this relative freedom he feels that there is a danger that an 'orthodoxy' will develop in art education, one which achieves the set targets with a minimal risk of failure but concurrently little sense of excitement or innovation. Although this study was conducted in 1994, the overall structure of education has not changed significantly in that time, suggesting that this opinion is still valid.

Pringle (2002) found that professional artists working in educational establishments embodied a conceptual approach both to the making and teaching of art (a pedagogy that has been highlighted as more easily facilitating the inclusion of contemporary art). As artists, as opposed to teachers, they work in this way in order to create supportive environments in which participants can be experimental. This way of working is not seen as a dissemination of skills and knowledge. The artists involved in the study saw the restrictions of the National Curriculum and timetable as prohibiting teachers from adopting this pedagogy within schools.

Long (2001) highlights again the extent to which the current structure of the National Curriculum can limit art education's ability to embrace new technologies and conceptual approaches. The multimedia project described in section A2, although successful, was limited in its potential by a lack of *departmental* resources. Access to the music department's equipment and to the expertise and facilities of the English and media departments could, it was felt, have extended this contemporary art project further. Aside from the lack of resources, this research also highlights a possible contextual factor that may be influencing the current status of contemporary art in secondary education. The current structure of the curriculum, which sees the art forms as separate identities, does not allow for the cross-curricular working in which contemporary art practice can flourish.

Long goes on to reinforce the earlier perspectives that the current structure of art education prevents teachers from developing new approaches to their teaching.

> *Amongst a number of perceived deficiencies within the learning taking place in classrooms were the narrow scope of work, the predictability of media and that students' outcomes were impersonal and preordained by teachers who did not feel able to take risks.*
> Long (2001, p.257)

A3.5 The implications of including contemporary art in the art curriculum

- What are the curriculum, assessment, staffing, training, resource and organisational implications of including contemporary art practice within school art?

The literature points to a small number of measures that may be required to overcome some of the barriers to the inclusion of contemporary art. (The literature addresses these as responses to the possible barriers considered in section A4, rather than presenting them as empirical research findings.) One of the main barriers presented is a lack of available and appropriate resources. Therefore, in order to include more contemporary art practice in the current curriculum, investments in resources would be needed. As highlighted by Callow (2001), Sinker (2001) and Loveless (2003) the introduction of new resources would need to be accompanied by adequate training for teachers in order for them to be able to incorporate them in to their teaching. Moreover, teachers' time would be needed in order for new resources, and therefore new practices, to be incorporated into existing schemes of work.

Rogers *et al.*, (2004) suggests that, while the provision and use of ICT in schools is expanding, the majority of art and design teachers do not feel confident in incorporating these technologies. As discussed in section A.3, this again highlights a need for adequate in-service training to accompany the new technologies that are becoming available to art departments.

Long (2001) goes as far as to suggest that a fundamental change in the way in which art is approached in schools would be needed to incorporate contemporary art practice fully. As discussed in section A4, he describes the current secondary curriculum structure as a barrier to art education. Whilst the art world is 'transgressing previously established boundaries' (Long, 2001, p.257) in its production of contemporary art, and young people are becoming familiar with multimedia approaches, school art is still operating under a segmentation of the art forms. In order to fully incorporate contemporary art practice into the secondary school curriculum, Long questions whether or not a return to an expressive arts department that is inclusive of all art forms, is in fact what is required.

The literature offers some implications that have resulted, or may result from the inclusion of contemporary art in school art. Whilst consistent in their findings, these are based on small scale research studies, or on author perspectives, and not on substantial empirical evidence. It is hoped that, by exploring examples of contemporary art practice in schools in the second phase of the research, more detailed implications will emerge.

A3.6 Perceptions of effects of incorporating contemporary art in the art curriculum

- What are teachers' and pupils' perceptions of the learning effects and outcomes of programmes involving contemporary art practice?
- Do they think that such programmes make a distinctive contribution to the curriculum and pupils' learning?

The majority of the research studies reviewed contain positive perceptions of the learning effects and outcomes of programmes involving contemporary art practice. For the most part they are small scale, cross-sectional projects and therefore it is difficult to ascertain perceptions of the overall contribution such programmes can make to the curriculum. However, there is some data concerned with the benefits to pupils' learning.

Long (2001) found that students enjoyed working with a new medium. Even within the short eight-month period of the project they began to broaden their own understanding of what constitutes art and how fine art and popular forms of media can be combined. Looking beyond this study, Long states that:

> *The need for children to develop a critical awareness of contemporary art through practical exploration and related contextual studies has become an established and valued element of art education.*
> Long (2001, p.257)

However, for the reasons cited in section A5, he concludes that this is only being partly met by current educational practices.

The perceptions of the benefits to be gained from contemporary art programmes are echoed in other small-scale projects. Teachers involved in the piloting of the DARE digital art resource (Sinker, 2001) were supportive of the access to contemporary art this provided for their students. They felt that discovering new and contemporary artists encouraged the students to think about the issues the artists were raising and to see art as a tool for addressing such issues. It also encouraged them to think more about the process and purpose of their own art work and develop a more conceptual approach as well as pushing them to explore new mediums. As in the latter research, accessing the DARE website appears to have widened the students' understanding of what 'art' can be.

Emery (2002b) concluded that teachers saw contemporary art as a way of showing the power of images as a medium for addressing social issues. The teachers in this study were starting to introduce a more issue-based approach to their art programmes and saw contemporary art, 'art that is a semblance of real life', as a tool for raising complex debates and for dealing with issues in the classroom.

> *...if controversial art works are avoided, teaching programmes fail to recognise the real-life issues that are the substance of much contemporary art.*
> Emery (2002b, p.7)

This perspective of the learning outcomes achievable through contemporary art may also be seen as having implications for citizenship education.

The overall perceptions of the teachers involved in the research reviewed have been positive. However, it might be assumed that these are studies involving teachers pre-disposed to the inclusion of contemporary art. Learning outcomes centre around the ability contemporary art has for developing students' conceptions of what art is and what it can do. The benefits are perceived in terms of how contemporary practice can improve students' critical awareness and conceptual thinking, as opposed to their art skills or their ability to produce 'good' art.

Alongside the recognised values of arts education, contemporary art practice is cited as key in assisting the desire both of education and art practitioners to address social change. Art education that embraces new technologies is viewed by a number of authors as instrumental in encouraging students to see art in the wider context of the world around them.

> *Arts education, particularly in a new relationship with science and technology, can address the need for creativity, the need of young people to be self motivated and confident, the need for the curriculum that prepares children for the modern world of mass communication and information technology.*
> Baynes (2000, p.42)

Burgess (2003) suggests that the inclusion of contemporary art may provide students with 'an opportunity to confront important personal, social and cultural issues'. By excluding contemporary art, which deals with real life, if sometimes controversial issues, the art curriculum fails to represent the world in which the students live. By including contemporary art and allowing students to engage with the 'potentially problematic' issues raised in contemporary art, the teacher can create an environment for discussion.

> *Teachers must look critically at pedagogic practices that promote fixity and deny students the opportunity to interrogate their immediate cultural environment.*
> Burgess (2003, p.109)

No data was found concerning pupils' perceptions of the outcomes of contemporary art-based programmes. The NFER main research hopes to ascertain the perceptions of pupils studying art in schools identified as incorporating contemporary art practices.

A3.7 Future prospects for including contemporary art in the school art curriculum

- What strategies might increase the potential for contemporary art practice to enhance the school art curriculum?

Despite positive data highlighting the reasons for including contemporary art, there is very little evidence within the literature reviewed on how to achieve this. Examples of possible strategies emerge from the smaller scale research projects reviewed. For example, Bloxham and Wass (2001) describe an approach to GCSE art employed in one school. The students were required to choose an artist or genre of their choice and explore this through project work. This improved the students' abilities to assess works of art critically, but also allowed them to access more controversial and obscure artists, who were of personal interest to them. In this case pupils chose to include a number of contemporary artists and art works. By allowing students a choice in areas, such as critical studies, it may be possible for students to look beyond the more traditional art present in the school curriculum.

Clive and Geggie (1998) suggest that education packs produced by museums and galleries are often used by teachers as a reference resource in schools, particularly when they contain information on more obscure artists and less traditional art forms, which it is difficult to find elsewhere.

> *Is there a point in producing a pack about Monet? You can get an interesting pack about Monet but it would be much better if money was spent on doing a pack on a contemporary artist, women artists, black artists...*
> Clive and Geggie (1998, p.51)

The research also includes suggestions for the future development of this relationship. It highlights the importance to galleries and museums of viewing school groups as significant audiences and planning exhibitions and associated work with this in mind. It is feasible that, by accessing artists or organisations that operate within the framework of the professional art world, students and schools can be made aware of issues, practice and developments within contemporary art that might otherwise be ignored.

Sekules (2003) also explores the potential role of art galleries in the teaching of the visual art curriculum through her work with the Sainsbury's Centre for Visual Arts at the University of East Anglia, and the 'Teachers in Service Training for Visual Arts' project. Whilst schools and teachers have legal requirements to show aims and objectives and to demonstrate improved standards (highlighted in section A4 as an inhibitor to the inclusion of contemporary art), art galleries operating in educational contexts are not necessarily constricted by the same guidelines. Therefore, Sekules suggests that galleries are more likely to develop an educational ethos based on questioning orthodox views of art. Modern artists and contemporary art galleries embrace the notion of pushing forward the boundaries and questioning the norm. By encouraging schools to work with galleries Sekules suggests an opportunity for accessing contemporary art and contemporary art practice in schools could then develop. Whilst 'getting an artist in' or visiting a gallery is not unusual for schools, Sekules comments that this is normally a one-off experience. By working in closer partnership with galleries and artists, schools may be able to begin to share in the culture of questioning aesthetic values that the 'contemporary culture of modern art and galleries promotes.'

The Ofsted perspective on school gallery visits (Ofsted, 2003), notes that current gallery usage is patchy in terms both of quality and quantity. However, inspection findings did reveal that such visits, when undertaken by schools, can 'raise pupils' awareness of contemporary art' and 'challenge accepted views [of art]'. As discussed by Sekules (2003), the Ofsted findings highlight the need for bespoke experiences in which schools and galleries collaborate in the planning of visits, and work in partnership in delivering an educational experience to the pupils.

Addison and Burgess (2003) suggest that PGCE students training as secondary art teachers could operate as 'agents of change' in bringing about a more contemporary approach to school art at key stages 3 and 4. They argue that secondary art PGCE students embark on their courses with the desire to deliver a new and innovative curriculum.

> *They begin the PGCE course fired up by the desire to reconceptualise the art curriculum so that it engages with contemporary culture and subject knowledge in the expanded field.*
> Addison and Burgess (2003a, p.160)

However, practice in their placement schools often conflicts with this ideology and there is pressure on them to recreate school orthodoxies.

> *In schools, especially at key stage 3, they often find a restricted curriculum, one squeezed of resources, with management demanding pretty pictures for the walls and a site where even the 'un-academic' pupil is expected to achieve a degree of success.*
> Addison and Burgess (2003a, p.160)

Addison and Burgess argue that, because of the enthusiasm for developing new pedagogical approaches to art and their position as 'the bridge between classroom pragmatism and the not yet possible', PGCE students are ideally placed to challenge existing orthodoxies. By questioning traditional approaches and instigating discussions with colleagues in schools they can open up the arena for discussions on the content and pedagogical approaches associated with traditional 'school art'.

> *Dialectic processes no doubt produce tensions, but they also prevent stagnation in the form of rigid orthodoxies.*
> Addison and Burgess (2003a, p.163)

The National Strategy for Education Art and Design (NSEAD), with financial support from ACE, established a national scheme of CPD for art teachers. The scheme is designed to develop collaborative working between educational institutions and galleries, and museums of contemporary art and is open to all art teachers and trainee art teachers. Programmes of study range from five-day intensive workshops through to part-time MAs, all with a specific focus on modern and contemporary art. Each of the seven educational institutions involved in the scheme determines its own structure and content for the courses offered. However, underlying each programme is an intention to provide participant teachers with '…opportunities to extend their awareness of the richness and complexity of fine art practice and of the diversity of thinking and influences which inform it'.

It is hoped that this scheme will provide the type of professional development not readily available to art teachers, and provide them with the enthusiasm, and the skills and knowledge, to incorporate contemporary art practice into their own teaching.

The literature provides limited concrete ideas for the inclusion of contemporary art practice in secondary art. As examined in section A2, these tend to be in the form of small, one-off projects rather than strategies for inclusion in the wider curriculum as a whole. As discussed, strategies for the inclusion of contemporary art can seek to go beyond singular schemes of work or lesson plans, and may need to have implications for the curriculum structure as a whole and for the way in which art, media and visual culture are addressed within education. Strategies designed to facilitate the inclusion of contemporary art have begun to be investigated. However, the way in which this inclusion can be fully utilised to support student learning has not been the subject of research to date, and would appear to be an issue for art educators in the future.

The NFER main research phase will hope to uncover further possible strategies for the inclusion of contemporary art practice, including the role of in-service training for teachers and the use of galleries and external artists, and will seek to provide evidence on how these can be developed.

A4 Conclusion

The literature review sought to address three broad questions, as summed up below.

A4.1 What is 'school art' at key stages 3 and 4?

The findings within the literature relating to a definition of 'school art' are limited. If 'school art' is defined separately from the art education employed by galleries, art organisations and non-teaching practitioners, then the National Curriculum requirements and associated guidelines can be seen, to an extent, as the defining documentation on what 'school art' is. However, as the studies included in the review suggest, educators are constantly looking at new ways of working in the arts, and of identifying what should be included within the prescribed framework. More research is needed in order to establish a national picture of what constitutes 'school art' at key stages 3 and 4.

A4.2 What are its main foci and contents?

Very little empirical evidence has been gathered to ascertain the main foci and content of school art. As in section A4.1, clues to actual practice can be drawn from QCA and other relevant documentation. QCA schemes of work are limited in their specific inclusion of contemporary media such as ICT and digital photography, as well as the exploration of contemporary art works. However, these are guidelines only and curriculum content employed to meet the National Curriculum objectives is open to teachers' individual discretion.

Factors that may influence curriculum content in visual arts are identified within the literature as the availability of resources, teacher expertise and the accessibility and adaptability of various art forms, including contemporary art. Time constraints and National Curriculum pressures are cited as possible reasons for focusing on more knowledge and skills-based pedagogies. Creativity and conceptual based foci are seen as needing more time and are more problematic in relation to assessment objectives.

A4.3 In what ways are pupils encouraged to broaden their approaches to the process of engaging with art forms and genres?

As discussed, the body of research reviewed concentrates on the types of media in which pupils work, particularly new media, and for the most part is not concerned with the processes involved in engaging with these. The media selected for inclusion in the curriculum can again be attributed to the resources available and the areas of expertise of the teaching staff. Multimedia approaches require sophisticated (and expensive) equipment and require teachers to be trained to use it (Callow, 2001). Art rooms, for the most part, are still designed for the traditional mediums of drawing and painting on paper and not for 3D or installation work, which require more flexible and spacious art rooms (Rogers and Bacon, 2002).

It appears, from the literature available, that the new areas being explored in secondary art education are based around the inclusion of ICT in art. Examples include digital photographs, graphic-based work and the manipulation of digital imagery. A significant number of small-scale action-based research projects are available, exploring how and why to incorporate ICT. The literature searches did not reveal any such projects looking at other contemporary media such as installation or 3D work.

It is difficult, from the literature reviewed, to draw any conclusions about the way in which more traditional media are being explored in new ways, within the curriculum. Nor does it allow conclusions to be drawn concerning the ways in which contemporary creative processes are being employed to encourage pupils to engage both with traditional and contemporary media.

To conclude, the following points can be deduced from the literature reviewed:

A4.4 The current status of contemporary art in the art curriculum

Very little empirical, large scale research has been conducted into the content of the school art curriculum at key stages 3 and 4. Research into the arts and visual art in education concentrates, for the most part, on the place of the arts within the curriculum, teachers' and managers' attitudes towards the arts, and perceptions of the benefits of arts teaching as a whole.

Evidence emerged from these studies to suggest that visual art education had moved away from conceptual approaches and more emphasis was being placed on the teaching of specific skills and knowledge. Because of the limited research available, it is difficult to ascertain the extent to which contemporary art is included in the curriculum. Examples in the literature reviewed document the use of ICT and digital technologies in the classroom as methods of including contemporary art. These were one-off projects and, although they raise some important issues, they provide little evidence about the ways in which contemporary art can become an integral part of the school curriculum.

A4.5 Barriers to the inclusion of contemporary art

The physical barriers to the inclusion of contemporary art in schools emerged as limited available resources (including information on contemporary artists and art works) and a lack of appropriate spaces (including art specific ICT suites) in which to explore new ways of working.

A number of contextual factors also emerged, which were seen as contributing to reluctance amongst teachers to include contemporary art. The present climate of assessment and target-driven education is seen as one of the key influencing factors, preventing teachers from taking risks and exploring more innovative art works.

QCA, AQA and other related documentation does not actively discourage the inclusion of contemporary art, nor does it actively promote it. Overall, the National Curriculum was perceived as a flexible framework in which teachers were free to design their own curriculum. Other contextual factors, for example, the 'weight of heritage' attached to art education, was seen as responsible for any lack of contemporary practice.

A4.6 Perception of the benefits of arts programmes including contemporary art

Despite the negative barriers emerging from the studies, there is a general consensus that contemporary art programmes can be of great benefit to pupils, though the evidence base for substantiating this remains limited. Individual projects have cited different outcomes, but overall it is felt that contemporary art can help to develop pupils' perceptions of what art is and of the role art plays in wider society and how it can be used to address social issues.

Contemporary art can also help to develop pupils' critical thinking skills. As they are faced with images they are unfamiliar with, including conceptual and abstract art, they are encouraged to think about the purpose, processes and overall effectiveness of the art works in question.

A4.7 The future inclusion of contemporary art in the art curriculum

Strategies for the future inclusion of contemporary art in the school curriculum emerged as continuations and developments of existing strategies, such as the increased use of professional artists and more collaboration between galleries and schools. Arguments also emerged to suggest that initial teacher training and CPD for art teachers could play an important role in challenging existing orthodoxies.

By bringing the evidence together, it is possible to suggest that any real change in the status and position of contemporary art in the school curriculum is dependent not only on increased resources and specific schemes of work, but also on a shift in the pedagogies employed. Pedagogies that adopt a more creative and cognitive approach, perhaps inclusive of multi-arts working, are seen as more easily adaptable to the genre of contemporary art.

Library search strategy

Database searches

A range of different educational, sociological and psychological databases were searched. Search strategies for all databases were developed by using terms from the relevant thesauri (where these were available), in combination with free text searching. The same search strategies were adhered to as far as possible for all the databases. The NFER library's own internal databases were also searched, as well as CERUK (Current Educational Research in the United Kingdom).

The database searches were supplemented by scanning the reference lists of relevant articles, thus identifying further studies. The team also searched relevant websites and downloaded documents and publications lists.

The bibliographic details of all papers identified through database searches and the potentially relevant papers found by hand, website and bibliography searching and through personal contact were entered onto a ProCite bibliographic database.

The keywords used in the database searches, together with a brief description of each of the databases searched, are outline below. All searches date from January 1989 to June 2004.

Australian education index (AEI)

AEI is produced by the Australian Council for Educational Research. It is an index to materials at all levels of education and related fields. Source documents include journal articles, monographs, research reports, theses, conference papers, legislation, parliamentary debates and newspaper articles.

 #1 Art* Education
 #2 Art* and Education
 #3 Design Education
 #4 Visual Arts
 #5 Contemporary Art*

#6	Performing Art*
#7	#1 or #2 or #3 or #4 or #5 or #6
#8	Secondary Education
#9	#7 and #8

British education index (BEI)

BEI provides bibliographic references to 350 British and selected European English-language periodicals in the field of education and training, plus developing coverage of national reports and conference literature.

#1	Arts Education
#2	Art Education
#3	Art$
#4	Design Education
#5	Visual Arts
#6	Contemporary Art$ (ft)
#7	Performing Art$ (ft)
#8	#1 or #2 or #3 or #4 or #5 or #6 or #7
#9	Primary Secondary Education
#10	Middle School Education
#11	Secondary Education
#12	#9 or # #10 or #11
#13	#8 and #12

| (ft) | Denotes free-text searching |
| $ | Denotes truncation of terms |

British education internet resource catalogue

The catalogue provides descriptions and hyperlinks for evaluated internet resources within an indexed database. The collection aims to list and describe significant information resources and services specifically relevant to the study, practice and administration of education at a professional level.

- #1   Arts Education
- #2   Arts
- #3   Art
- #4   Art Education
- #5   Design Education
- #6   Contemporary Arts
- #7   Visual Arts
- #8   Performing Arts

Canadian business and current affairs (CBCA)

CBCA provides indexing and full text access to the principal educational literature publications in Canada, covering all significant reports of government departments, faculties of education, teachers' associations, large school boards and educational organisations. Over 150 educational periodicals, plus educational articles in over 700 general journals and newspapers are indexed.

- #1   Arts Education
- #2   Design Education
- #3   Visual Art*
- #4   Contemporary Art*
- #5   Performing Art*
- #6   #1 or #2 or #3 or #4 or #5
- #7   Secondary Education
- #8   #6 and #7

ChildData

ChildData is the National Children's Bureau database containing details of around 35,000 books, reports and journal articles about children and young people.

Searches date from 1989–2003.

#1	Art
#2	Education
#3	#1 and #2

ERIC

ERIC is sponsored by the United States Department of Education and is the largest education database in the world. It indexes over 725 periodicals and currently contains more than 7,000,000 records. Coverage includes research documents, journal articles, technical reports, programme descriptions and evaluations and curriculum material. Searches date from 1989–2003.

#1	Art Education
#2	Design Education (ft)
#3	Visual Art?
#4	Contemporary Art? (ft)
#5	Theatre Arts
#6	#1 or #2 or #3 or #4 or #5
#7	Secondary Education
#8	#6 and #7
$	Denotes truncation of terms

Websites

ADAM   The gateway to Art, Design, Architecture and Media information on the internet

AHDS   The Arts and Humanities Data Service

NSEAD The National Society for Education in Art and Design

Appendix 2 Images used during research

Image 1
Andrew Thompson
(Corstorphine Primary School, working
with Stills Gallery, Edinburgh, 2000).
Message for the Future.
Winner of the Chrisi Bailey Award 2000.

Image 2
David Shrigley
Terrible News – no more treats!
From 'Blank Page and Other Pages'
1998
© the artist

Image 3
Richard Billingham
Untitled
1995
© the artist

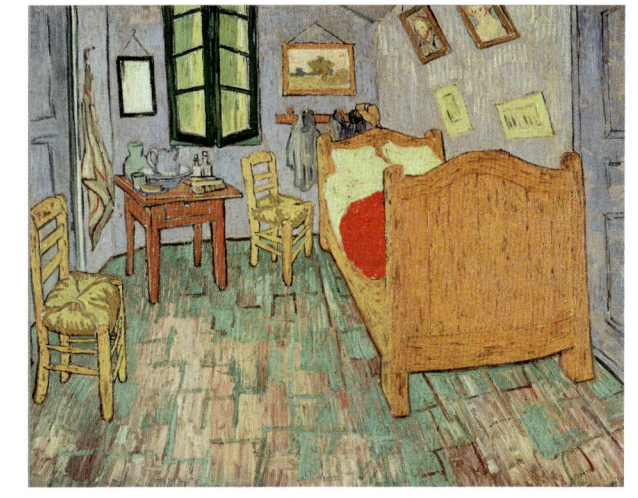

Image 4
Vincent Van Gogh
Van Gogh's Bedroom at Arles
1889
Art Institute of Chicago

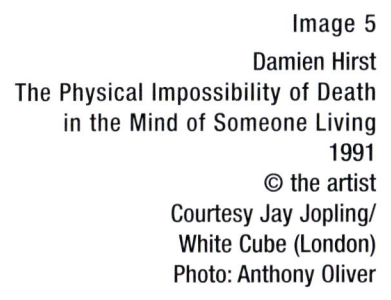

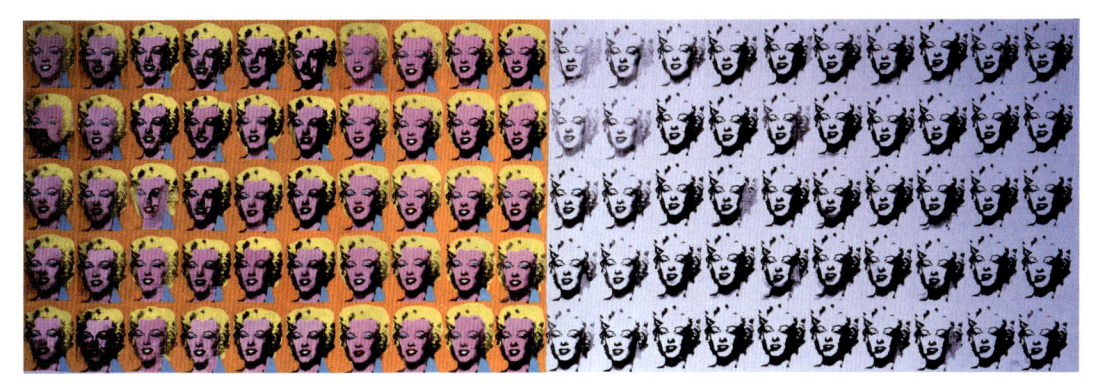

Image 5
Damien Hirst
The Physical Impossibility of Death
in the Mind of Someone Living
1991
© the artist
Courtesy Jay Jopling/
White Cube (London)
Photo: Anthony Oliver

Image 6
Andy Warhol
Marilyn x 100
1962
The Cleveland Museum of Art
© The Andy Warhol Foundation for the Visual Arts, Inc./
ARS, NY and DACS, London 2004-10-29
TM 2004 Marilyn Monroe, LLC by CMG Worldwide, Inc./
www.MarilynMonroe.com

References

ADDISON, N. and BURGESS, L. (2003). 'Challenging orthodoxies through partnership.' In: ADDISON, N. and BURGESS, L. (Eds) *Issues in Art and Design Teaching*. London: Routledge.

ASSESSMENT AND QUALIFICATIONS ALLIANCE (2002). *General Certificate of Education, Art and Design: Specifications for Examination in 2004 Onwards*. Exeter: Assessment and Qualifications Alliance.

BARRETT, M. (1990). 'Art, craft and design and the National Curriculum', *Education 3–13*, **18**, 3, 46–9.

BAYNES, K. (2000). 'Gallery of the future: new directions in arts education', *International Journal of Art & Design Education*, **19**, 1, 37–43.

BINCH, N. (1994). 'The implications of the National Curriculum orders for art for GCSE and beyond', *Journal of Art & Design Education*, **13**, 2, 117–31.

BLOXHAM, A. and WASS, K. (2001). 'The trouble with GCSE and critical studies', *International Journal of Art & Design Education*, **20**, 1, 49–56.

BURGESS, L. (2003). 'Monsters in the playground: including contemporary art.' In: ADDISON, N. and BURGESS, L. (Eds) *Issues in Art and Design Teaching*. London: Routledge.

CALLOW, P. (2001). 'ICT in art', *International Journal of Art & Design Education*, **20**, 1, 41–8.

CLIVE, S. and GEGGIE, P. (1998). *Unpacking Teachers' Packs*. London: Engage.

DEARING, R. (1994). *The National Curriculum and Its Assessment: Final Report*. London: SCAA.

EMERY, L. (2002a). 'Censorship in contemporary art education', *International Journal of Art & Design Education*, **1**, 1, 5–13.

EMERY, L. (2002b). *Teaching Art in a Post-modern World*. Melbourne: Common Ground Publishing .

HARGREAVES, D.J. and LAMONT, A. (2002). *Investigation of a Randomly Stratified Sample of Schools by the Universities of Surrey Roehampton and Keele* [online]. Available: http://www.qca.org.uk/artsalive/why_invest/stratified_report.htm [2 August, 2004].

HARLAND, J., KINDER, K., LORD, P., STOTT, A., SCHAGEN, I. and HAYNES, J. with CUSWORTH, L., WHITE, R. and PAOLA, R. (2000). *Arts Education in Secondary Schools: Effects and Effectiveness.* Slough: NFER.

HUGHES, A. (1998). 'Reconceptualising the art curriculum', *Journal of Art & Design Education,* **17**, 1, 41–9.

HULKS, D. (2003). 'Measuring artistic performance: the assessment debate and art education.' In: ADDISON, N. and BURGESS, L. (Eds) *Issues in Art and Design Teaching.* London: Routledge.

HUTCHINSON, M. (1998). 'Of monsterology.' In: McCORQUODALE, D., SIDERFIN, N. and STALLABRASS, J. (Eds) *Occupational Hazard: Critical Writing on Recent British Art.* London: Black Dog. Cited in: BURGESS, L. (2003). 'Monsters in the playground: including contemporary art.' In: ADDISON, N. and BURGESS, L. (Eds) *Issues in Art and Design Teaching.* London: Routledge.

LONG, S. (2001). 'Multimedia in the art curriculum: crossing boundaries', *International Journal of Art & Design Education,* **20**, 3, 255–63.

LOVELESS, A. (2003). 'Making a difference? An evaluation of professional knowledge and pedagogy in art and ICT', *Journal of Art & Design Education,* **22**, 2, 145–54.

OFFICE FOR STANDARDS IN EDUCATION (2001). *Inspecting Art and Design: 11–16 with Guidance on Self-evaluation.* London: OFSTED.

OFFICE FOR STANDARDS IN EDUCATION (2003). *Making Effective Use of Galleries: Ofsted Subject Reports Conference Series 2002/03* (HMI 1641). London: OFSTED.

PRINGLE, E. (2002). *'We Did Stir Things Up': the Role of Artists in Sites for Learning.* London: The Arts Council England.

QUALIFICATIONS AND CURRICULUM AUTHORITY (2003a). *Art and Design at Key Stage 3, Unit 8b: Animating Art* [online]. Available: http://www.standards.dfes.gov.uk/schemes2/secondary_art/art08b/ [2 August, 2004].

QUALIFICATIONS AND CURRICULUM AUTHORITY (2003b). *Art and Design at Key Stage 3, Unit 9b: Change your Style* [online]. Available: http://www.standards.dfes.gov.uk/schemes2/secondary_art/art09b/ [2 August, 2004].

QUALIFICATIONS AND CURRICULUM AUTHORITY (2003c). *The National Curriculum Online. Programme of Study: Art and Design Key Stage 3* [online]. Available: http://www.nc.uk.net/nc/contents/AD-3--POS.html [3 August, 2004].

ROGERS, R. and BACON, S. (Eds) (2002). *Space for Art: a Handbook for Creative Learning Environments*. London: Clore Duffield Foundation.

ROGERS, R., EDWARDS, S. and GODFREY, F. (2004). *State of the Art*. London: Clore Duffield Foundation.

ROSS, M. and KAMBA, M. (1997). *The State of the Arts in Five English Secondary Schools*. Exeter: University of Exeter, School of Education.

SEKULES, V. (2003). 'The celebrity performer and the creative facilitator: the artist, the school and the museum.' In: XANTHOUDAKI, M., TICKLE, L. and SEKULES, V. (Eds) *Researching Visual Arts Education in Museums and Galleries*. Dordrecht: Kluwer Academic Press.

SINKER, R. (2001). 'Distance no object: developing DARE, the Digital Art Resource for Education', *International Journal of Art & Design Education*, **20**, 1, 31–40.

Further Reading

ADDISON, N. (1999). 'Who's afraid of signs and significations? Defending semiotics in the secondary art and design curriculum', *Journal of Art & Design Education*, **18**, 1, 33–9.

ADDISON, N. and BURGESS, L. (Eds) (2003). Issues in Art and Design Teaching. London: Routledge.

ALLISON, B. and HAUSMAN, J. (1998). 'The limits of theory in art education', *Journal of Art & Design Education*, **17**, 2, 121–7.

ATKINSON, D. (1995). 'Discourse and practice in the art curriculum and the production of the pupil as a subject', *Journal of Art & Design Education*, **14**, 3, 259–70.

ATKINSON, D. (1999). 'A critical reading of the National Curriculum for art in the light of contemporary theories of subjectivity', *Journal of Art & Design Education*, **18**, 1, 107–13.

ATKINSON, D. (2001). 'Assessment in educational practice: forming pedagogised identities in the art curriculum', *International Journal of Art & Design Education*, **20**, 1, 96–108.

CLARK, R.A. (1993). 'Beyond visual arts: the importance of nomenclature', *Canadian Society for Education Through Art*, **24**, 1, 12–16.

DASH, P. (1999). 'Thoughts on a relevant art curriculum for the 21st century', *Journal of Art & Design Education*, **18**, 1, 123–7.

DUNCUM, P. (1996). 'Beyond the fine art ghettos: why the visual arts are important in education', *Canadian Review of Art Education*, **23**, 1, 72–5.

DUNCUM, P. (2002). 'Visual culture art education: why, what and how', *International Journal of Art & Design Education*, **21**, 1, 14–23.

HOBBS, T., CONNELL, P. and HAIS, L. (2000). *Evaluation of the Years 1 to 10, the Arts Curriculum Development Project, Report 3*. Queensland: Queensland School Curriculum Council.

HUGHES, A. (1999). 'Art and intention in schools: towards a new paradigm', *Journal of Art & Design Education*, **18**, 1, 129–34.

MacDONALD, S. (1993). 'A National Curriculum or national guidelines for art and design 5–14?' *Journal of Art & Design Education*, **12**, 1, 25–39.

PARKER, D. (2001). 'Moving image media and future illiteracies: the role of cineliteracy in curriculum development', *International Journal of Art & Design Education*, **20**, 3, 296–301.

RAYMENT, T. (1999). 'Assessing National Curriculum art AT2, knowledge and understanding: a small-scale project at key stage 3', *Journal of Art & Design Education*, **18**, 2, 189–94.

ROGERS, R., EDWARDS, S. and STEERS, J. (2001). *Survey of Art and Design Resources in Primary and Secondary Schools*. London: Clore Duffield Foundation.

SEKULES, V. and XANTHOUDAKI, M. (Eds) (2003). *The Teacher, the School and the Museum*. Milan: Socrates Project.

SWIFT, J. (1999). 'Institutional art education: curriculum, teacher and learner', *Journal of Art & Design Education*, **18**, 1, 99–106.